Rick Steves ®

SNAPSHOT

Dublin

CONTENTS

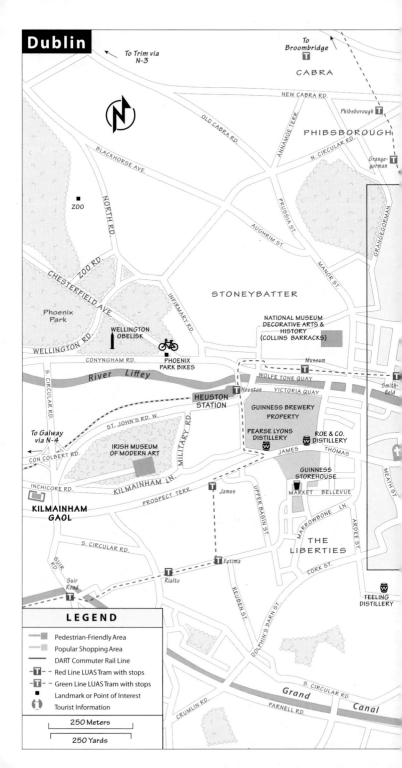

Dublin

To Trim via N-3

CABRA

To Broombridge

NEW CABRA RD.

OLD CABRA RD.

Phibsborough

PHIBSBOROUGH

BLACKHORSE AVE.

ANNAMOE TERR.

N. CIRCULAR RD.

Grange-gorman

ZOO

NORTH RD.

PRUSSIA ST.

AUGHRIM ST.

MANOR ST.

GRANGEGORMAN

ZOO RD.

CHESTERFIELD AVE.

STONEYBATTER

Phoenix Park

INFIRMARY RD.

NATIONAL MUSEUM DECORATIVE ARTS & HISTORY (COLLINS BARRACKS)

WELLINGTON RD.

WELLINGTON OBELISK

PHOENIX PARK BIKES

Museum

CONYNGHAM RD.

River Liffey

Smith-field

Heuston

WOLFE TONE QUAY

VICTORIA QUAY

S. CIRCULAR RD.

HEUSTON STATION

GUINNESS BREWERY PROPERTY

ST. JOHN'S RD. W.

MILITARY RD.

PEARSE LYONS DISTILLERY

ROE & CO. DISTILLERY

To Galway via N-4

IRISH MUSEUM OF MODERN ART

JAMES

THOMAS

CON COLBERT RD.

KILMAINHAM LN.

GUINNESS STOREHOUSE

MEATH ST.

INCHICORE RD.

PROSPECT TERR.

James

UPPER BASIN ST.

MARKET

BELLEVUE

KILMAINHAM GAOL

S. CIRCULAR RD.

MARROWBONE LN.

ARDEE ST.

THE LIBERTIES

SUIR RD.

Fatima

CORK ST.

Suir Road

Rialto

REUBEN ST.

TEELING DISTILLERY

DOLPHIN'S BARN ST.

CRUMLIN RD.

PARNELL RD.

S. CIRCULAR RD.

Grand Canal

LEGEND

- Pedestrian-Friendly Area
- Popular Shopping Area
- DART Commuter Rail Line
- Red Line LUAS Tram with stops
- Green Line LUAS Tram with stops
- Landmark or Point of Interest
- Tourist Information

250 Meters

250 Yards

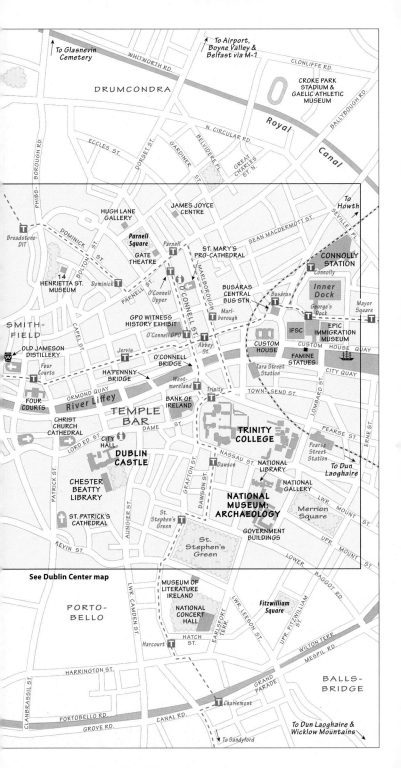

To Glasnevin Cemetery

To Airport,
Boyne Valley &
Belfast via M-1

WHITWORTH RD.

CLONLIFFE RD.

DRUMCONDRA

CROKE PARK
STADIUM &
GAELIC ATHLETIC
MUSEUM

Royal

N. CIRCULAR RD.

Canal

ECCLES ST.

BELVIDERE PL.

GREAT
CHARLES
ST. N.

DORSET ST.

GARDINER ST.

BALLYBOUGH RD.

PHIBS-
BOROUGH RD.

Broadstone-
DIT

DOMINICK ST.

BOLTON ST.

CAPEL ST.

HUGH LANE
GALLERY

JAMES JOYCE
CENTRE

SEAN MACDERMOTT ST.

SEVILLE PL.

To
Howth

Parnell
Square

Parnell

ST. MARY'S
PRO-CATHEDRAL

CONNOLLY
STATION

Connolly

GATE
THEATRE

Parnell St.

Inner
Dock

14
HENRIETTA ST.
MUSEUM

Dominick

O'Connell
Upper

MARLBOROUGH ST.

BUSÁRAS
CENTRAL
BUS STN.

Busáras

George's
Dock

Mayor
Square

PARNELL ST.

SMITH-
FIELD

GPO WITNESS
HISTORY EXHIBIT

O'CONNELL ST.

Marl-
borough

CUSTOM
HOUSE

IFSC

EPIC
IMMIGRATION
MUSEUM

CUSTOM
HOUSE QUAY

OLD JAMESON
DISTILLERY

O'Connell GPO

Abbey
St.

Jervis

O'CONNELL
BRIDGE

Tara Street
Station

FAMINE
STATUES

CITY QUAY

Four
Courts

HA'PENNY
BRIDGE

West-
moreland

LOMBARD ST.

ERNE ST.

ORMOND QUAY

River Liffey

BANK OF
IRELAND

Trinity

TOWN-SEND ST.

FOUR
COURTS

TEMPLE
BAR

DAME ST.

Westmoreland

PEARSE ST.

CHRIST
CHURCH
CATHEDRAL

LORD ED. ST.

CITY
HALL

TRINITY
COLLEGE

Pearse
Street
Station

PATRICK ST.

DUBLIN
CASTLE

Dawson

NASSAU ST.

NATIONAL
LIBRARY

To Dun
Laoghaire

CHESTER
BEATTY
LIBRARY

GRAFTON ST.

DAWSON ST.

NATIONAL
GALLERY

MOUNT ST.

ST. PATRICK'S
CATHEDRAL

AUNGIER ST.

NATIONAL
MUSEUM:
ARCHAEOLOGY

Merrion
Square

LWR. MOUNT ST.

KEVIN ST.

St.
Stephen's
Green

GOVERNMENT
BUILDINGS

UPR. MOUNT ST.

St. Stephen's
Green

LOWER

BAGGOT RD.

See Dublin Center map

PORTO-
BELLO

LWR. CAMDEN ST.

MUSEUM OF
LITERATURE
IRELAND

NATIONAL
CONCERT
HALL

EARLSFORT TERR.

LWR. LEESON ST.

Fitzwilliam
Square

UPR. FITZWILLIAM ST.

BALLS-
BRIDGE

Harcourt

HATCH
ST.

WILTON TERR.

MESPIL RD.

CLANBRASSIL ST.

HARRINGTON ST.

GRAND
PARADE

PORTOBELLO RD.

Charlemont

Canal

GROVE RD.

To Sandyford

To Dun Laoghaire &
Wicklow Mountains

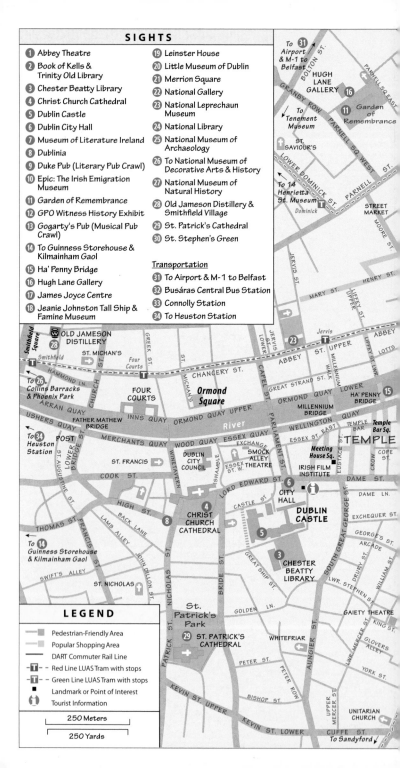

SIGHTS

1. Abbey Theatre
2. Book of Kells & Trinity Old Library
3. Chester Beatty Library
4. Christ Church Cathedral
5. Dublin Castle
6. Dublin City Hall
7. Museum of Literature Ireland
8. Dublinia
9. Duke Pub (Literary Pub Crawl)
10. Epic: The Irish Emigration Museum
11. Garden of Remembrance
12. GPO Witness History Exhibit
13. Gogarty's Pub (Musical Pub Crawl)
14. To Guinness Storehouse & Kilmainham Gaol
15. Ha' Penny Bridge
16. Hugh Lane Gallery
17. James Joyce Centre
18. Jeanie Johnston Tall Ship & Famine Museum
19. Leinster House
20. Little Museum of Dublin
21. Merrion Square
22. National Gallery
23. National Leprechaun Museum
24. National Library
25. National Museum of Archaeology
26. To National Museum of Decorative Arts & History
27. National Museum of Natural History
28. Old Jameson Distillery & Smithfield Village
29. St. Patrick's Cathedral
30. St. Stephen's Green

Transportation

31. To Airport & M-1 to Belfast
32. Busáras Central Bus Station
33. Connolly Station
34. To Heuston Station

LEGEND

- Pedestrian-Friendly Area
- Popular Shopping Area
- DART Commuter Rail Line
- T - Red Line LUAS Tram with stops
- T - Green Line LUAS Tram with stops
- ■ Landmark or Point of Interest
- Tourist Information

250 Meters
250 Yards

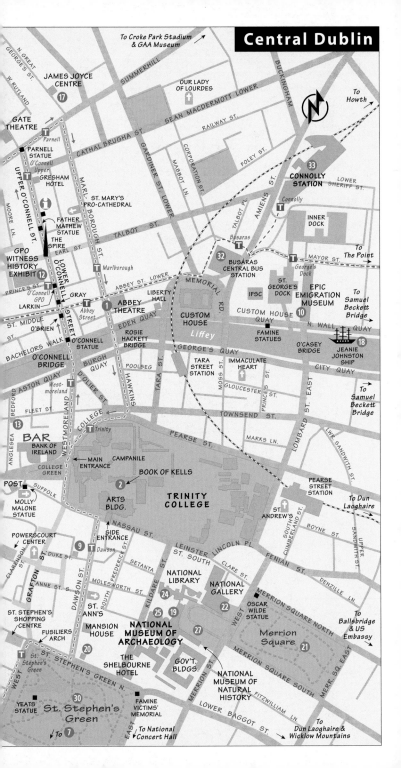

Central Dublin

To Croke Park Stadium & GAA Museum

To Howth

To The Point

To Samuel Beckett Bridge

To Samuel Beckett Bridge

To Dun Laoghaire

To Ballsbridge & US Embassy

To Dun Laoghaire & Wicklow Mountains

To National Concert Hall

To ⑦

JAMES JOYCE CENTRE ⑰

GATE THEATRE

OUR LADY OF LOURDES

SUMMERHILL

N. GREAT GEORGE'S ST.
W. RUTLAND
Parnell
PARNELL STATUE
O'Connell Upper
GRESHAM HOTEL
UPPER O'CONNELL ST.
MOORE LN.

SEAN MACDERMOTT LOWER
RAILWAY ST.
CATHAL BRUGHA ST.
GARDINER ST. LOWER
MARLBOROUGH ST.
CORPORATION ST.
MABBOT LN.
FOLEY ST.

BUCKINGHAM

CONNOLLY STATION ㉝
LOWER SHERIFF ST.
Connolly
INNER DOCK

ST. MARY'S PRO-CATHEDRAL
FATHER MATHEW STATUE
THE SPIRE
EARL ST.
Marlborough
LOWER O'CONNELL ST.
GPO WITNESS HISTORY EXHIBIT ⑫
PRINCE'S ST.
O'Connell GPO
LARKIN
ST. MIDDLE
O'BRIEN
BACHELORS WALK

TALBOT ST.
Busaras
Busáras
BUSÁRAS CENTRAL BUS STATION ㉜
MAYOR ST.
George's Dock
St. GEORGE'S DOCK
IFSC
CUSTOM HOUSE QUAY
N. WALL QUAY

EPIC EMIGRATION MUSEUM ⑩

TALBOT PL.
AMIENS ST.
MEMORIAL RD.

GRAY
ABBEY ST. LOWER
ABBEY THEATRE ①
LIBERTY HALL
CUSTOM HOUSE
Liffey
EDEN QUAY
ROSIE HACKETT BRIDGE
GEORGE'S QUAY
FAMINE STATUES
O'CASEY BRIDGE
CITY QUAY

O'CONNELL STATUE
O'CONNELL BRIDGE
BURGH QUAY
POOLBEG
TARA ST.
TARA STREET STATION
IMMACULATE HEART
GLOUCESTER ST.
PRINCE'S ST.

JEANIE JOHNSTON SHIP ⑱

BEDFORD
ASTON QUAY
Westmoreland
D'OLIER ST.
FLEET ST.
HAWKINS
TOWNSEND ST.
MARKS LN.
LOMBARD ST. EAST
LWR. SANDWITH ST.

⑬
BAR
BANK OF IRELAND
ANGLESEA
COLLEGE
Trinity
COLLEGE GREEN
MAIN ENTRANCE
CAMPANILE
BOOK OF KELLS
② **ARTS BLDG.**
TRINITY COLLEGE
PEARSE ST.
PEARSE STREET STATION
CUMBERLAND ST.
BOYNE ST.
SANDWITH ST.
UPPER SANDWITH ST.

POST
SUFFOLK
MOLLY MALONE STATUE
POWERSCOURT CENTER
⑨
CLARENDON ST.
S. DUKE ST.
Dawson
NASSAU ST.
SIDE ENTRANCE
LEINSTER ST. SOUTH
LINCOLN PL.
CLARE ST.
FENIAN ST.
DENZILLE LN.

To Dun Laoghaire

ST. ANDREW'S

GRAFTON ST.
ANNE ST. S.
S. FREDERICK ST.
SETANTA
MOLESWORTH ST.
KILDARE ST.
NATIONAL LIBRARY
㉔
NATIONAL GALLERY
㉒
OSCAR WILDE STATUE
MERRIN SQUARE NORTH
WEST

ST. STEPHEN'S SHOPPING CENTRE
FUSILIERS ARCH
ST. ANN'S
DAWSON ST.
㉕ ⑲
NATIONAL MUSEUM OF ARCHAEOLOGY
㉗
Merrion Square
㉑

MANSION HOUSE
⑳
THE SHELBOURNE HOTEL
GOV'T. BLDGS.
MERRION SQUARE SOUTH
MERR. SQ. EAST

ST. STEPHEN'S GREEN N.
WEST
ST. STEPHEN'S GREEN
YEATS STATUE
㉚
St. Stephen's Green
FAMINE VICTIMS' MEMORIAL
EAST
MERRION ST.
NATIONAL MUSEUM OF NATURAL HISTORY
FITZWILLIAM LN.
LOWER BAGGOT ST.
FITZWILLIAM

INTRODUCTION

This Snapshot guide, excerpted from my guidebook *Rick Steves Ireland,* introduces you to the city of Dublin. From its lively pubs filled with Guinness-fueled *craic* (conversation) and traditional music, to its stately Georgian sights, to its powerful rebel history, the Irish capital delights its visitors. Stroll vibrant O'Connell Street for a lesson in Ireland's long struggle for independence, cheer on the local hurling team at Croke Park, and pore over the intricately decorated ninth-century Book of Kells. Pious, earthy, witty, brooding, feisty, and unpretentious, Dublin is an intoxicating potion to sip or slurp—as the mood strikes you.

For a break from the big city, venture to sights near Dublin: the prehistoric tombs at Brú na Bóinne, the site of the pivotal Battle of the Boyne, the stout ruins of Trim Castle, the impressive Gardens of Powerscourt, the monastic settlement at Glendalough, and the proud Irish equestrian tradition at the National Stud.

To help you have the best trip possible, I've included the following topics in this book:

- **Planning Your Time,** with advice on how to make the most of your limited time
- **Orientation,** including tourist information (abbreviated as TI), tips on public transportation, local tour options, and helpful hints
- **Sights,** with ratings and strategies for meaningful and efficient visits
- **Sleeping** and **Eating,** with good-value recommendations in every price range
- **Connections,** with tips on trains, buses, and driving

Practicalities, near the end of this book, has information on money, staying connected, hotel reservations, transportation, and other helpful hints.

To travel smartly, read this little book in its entirety before you go. It's my hope that this guide will make your trip more meaningful and rewarding. Traveling like a temporary local, you'll get the absolute most out of every mile, minute, and dollar.

Happy travels!

Rick Steves

DUBLIN

With reminders of its stirring history and rich culture on every corner, Ireland's capital and largest city is a sightseer's delight. Boasting an excellent archaeology museum; the remarkable Book of Kells at Trinity College; a patriotic jail; and a thriving pub scene awash in Celtic music, storytelling, and Guinness, Dublin punches above its weight in arts, entertainment, food, and fun.

Founded as a Viking trading settlement in the ninth century, Dublin grew to be a center of wealth and commerce, second only to London in the British Empire. As the seat of English rule in Ireland for over 700 years, Dublin was the heart of the "civilized" Anglo-Irish area (eastern Ireland) known as "the Pale." Anything "beyond the Pale" was considered uncultured and almost barbaric... purely Irish.

The golden age of English Dublin was the 18th century. The British Empire was on a roll, and the city was right there with it. Largely rebuilt during this Georgian era (1714-1830), Dublin became elegant and cultured.

But the 19th century saw Ireland endure the Great Potato Famine, and tension with the British culminated in the Easter Rising of 1916, followed by a suc-cessful guerilla war of indepen-dence and Ireland's tragic civil war that left many of its grand streets in ruins.

While bullet-pocked build-ings and dramatic statues keep memories of Ireland's struggle for independence alive, today's

Dublin is lively, easy, and extremely accessible. The city's economy is on the upswing, with a forest of cranes sweeping over booming construction blocks and expanding light-rail infrastructure. Dubliners are energetic and helpful, and visitors enjoy a big-town cultural scene wrapped in a small-town smile.

DUBLIN

PLANNING YOUR TIME

While you could easily spend much longer here, for most Ireland vacations, Dublin merits three nights and two days. Here's how I would fill two days in Dublin:

Day 1

9:00	Follow my "Dublin City Walk" through the center of town, incorporating a visit to the GPO Witness History Museum (at the General Post Office in North Dublin)
13:00	Lunch
15:00	Visit EPIC: The Irish Emigration Museum, Chester Beatty Library, 14 Henrietta Street, or whichever sight interests you most
Evening	Do the Traditional Irish Musical Pub Crawl, the Literary Pub Crawl, or other evening show

Day 2

9:00	Tour Trinity College campus followed by a visit to the Book of Kells exhibit (book in advance)
11:00	Visit the National Museum of Archaeology
13:00	Lunch
15:00	Visit Kilmainham Gaol (book in advance)
Evening	Linger over dinner at one of Dublin's fine restaurants, or enjoy some live music at a pub

Orientation to Dublin

Greater Dublin sprawls with about 1.4 million people—about a third of the country's population. But the center of tourist interest is a tight triangle between O'Connell Bridge, St. Stephen's Green, and Christ Church Cathedral. Within or near this triangle, you'll find Trinity College (Book of Kells), a cluster of major museums (including the National Museum of Archaeology), touristy and pedestrianized Grafton Street, Temple Bar (touristy nightlife center), Dublin Castle, and the hub of most city tours and buses. Only two major sights are beyond easy walking distance from this central zone: Kilmainham Gaol and the Guinness Storehouse.

The River Liffey cuts the town in two, and most of your sightseeing will take place on its south bank. As you explore, be aware that many long Dublin streets change names every few blocks, including the wide main axis that cuts north/south through the tourist center. North from the O'Connell Bridge, it's called O'Connell Street; south of the bridge, it becomes Westmoreland, passes Trinity College, and becomes the pedestrian-only Grafton Street to St. Stephen's Green.

Two suburbs, Dun Laoghaire to the south and Howth to the north, offer quiet, less expensive home-base alternatives to Dublin (with frequent and easy transit connections into town).

TOURIST INFORMATION

Dublin's main TI, in South Dublin, has lots of info on Dublin and all of Ireland (on Barnardo Square next to City Hall, near Dublin Castle). A smaller TI is in North Dublin, just past the stainless-steel sculpture known as the Spire, on the east side of O'Connell Street (both branches open Mon-Sat 9:00-17:00, closed Sun, www.visitdublin.com). Beware of other shops claiming to be "Tourist Information" points, especially on O'Connell Street. Their advice is biased, aiming to sell you tours and collect commissions.

Sightseeing Passes: The **Dublin Pass** covers more than 35 sights, the hop-on, hop-off Big Bus, plus a few guided tours (€69/1 day, €89/2 days, more multiday options available, purchase online and download to your phone, https://dublinpass.com). Note that if you have the **Heritage Card** for Ireland, it covers two big Dublin sights (Kilmainham Gaol and Dublin Castle).

ARRIVAL IN DUBLIN

By Train: Dublin has two train stations, both with ATMs but no lockers.

Heuston Station, on the west end of town, serves west and southwest Ireland. Nearby baggage storage is at Tipperary House B&B (daily 8:00-20:00, 7 Parkgate Street, hidden beside huge Ashling Hotel visible from station, 5-minute walk from station, +353 1 679 5317, www.tipperaryhousedublin.com).

Connolly Station is closer to the center and serves the north, northwest, and Rosslare. There is baggage storage directly across the street from the station at an internet/shipping/call shop (daily 10:00-22:00, 16 Amiens Street, +353 1 537 7413).

If you're **changing trains** in Dublin, you may also change train stations. For example, to go from Belfast to Kilkenny you'll arrive at Connolly Station, then transfer to Heuston Station to catch the Kilkenny train. The two stations are best connected by the red line of the LUAS tram system (20-minute ride; see "Getting Around Dublin," later). Bus #90, which runs along the river (€1.70, 4/hour), also links the train stations.

By Bus: Bus Éireann, Ireland's national bus company, uses the Busáras Central Bus Station (pronounced bu-SAUR-us), located one block south of Connolly Station.

By Car: Don't drive in downtown Dublin—traffic's terrible and parking is expensive. If you must park in central Dublin, a good option is Q-Park Christ Church, on Werburgh Street behind Jurys Inn Christ Church (€4.30/hour, €39/24 hours, €14/overnight, +353 1 634 9805, www.q-park.ie). For more on driving, including Dublin's toll road, see "Dublin Connections" on page 95.

By Plane or Ferry: For details on Dublin's airport, UK ferries, and more, see "Dublin Connections" on page 95.

HELPFUL HINTS

Sightseeing Tips: Dublin can be crowded. Book in advance for the Book of Kells at Trinity College, the Guinness Storehouse, and Kilmainham Gaol. And, if you are set on any evening activity, tour, or fine meal, reservations are a must.

Pickpockets: Dublin is not immune to this scourge. Be on guard—use a money belt or carefully zip things up.

Festivals: St. Patrick's Day is a four-day March extravaganza in Dublin (www.stpatricksday.ie). June 16 is **Bloomsday,** dedicated to the Irish author James Joyce and featuring the Messenger Bike Rally (www.jamesjoyce.ie). Book hotels ahead during festivals and for any weekend (see more advice in the "Sleeping in Dublin" section).

Mass in Latin: The Roman Catholic Mass is said in Latin daily at St. Kevin's Church (Mon-Fri at 8:00, Sat at 9:00, Sun at 9:00 and 10:30, corner of Harrington and Synge, about 6 blocks south of St. Patrick's Cathedral, www.latinmassdublin.ie).

Laundry: Ask your hotelier for the nearest laundry. For full service laundry, try **Krystal Dry Cleaners,** a block southwest of Jurys Inn Christ Church on Patrick Street (Mon-Sat 8:00-19:00, Sun 12:00-17:00, +353 1 454 6864, www.krystaldrycleaners.com). The **All-American Launderette** offers both self- and full-service options (Mon-Sat 8:30-19:00, closed Sun, 40 South Great George's Street, +353 1 677 2779, www.allamericanlaunderette. com). For locations, see the map on page 84.

Bike Rental: Just inside Phoenix Park's main entrance is **Phoenix Park Bikes**—a great place to start a low-stress ride into the huge, bike-friendly park (standard bikes—€7/1 hour, €14/3 hours, €20/day, e-bikes are double these rates, all rentals include helmets, open daily 10:00-17:00, longer Sat-Sun hours in summer—9:00-20:00, north side of the Liffey on Chester-

DUBLIN

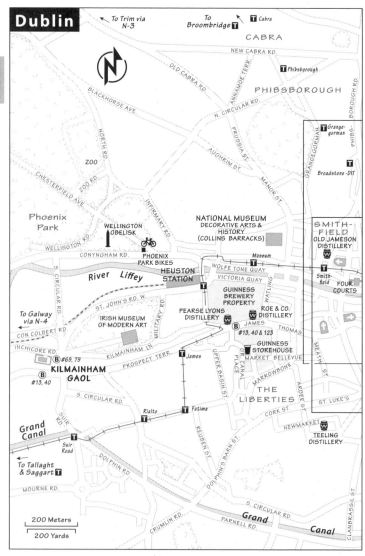

field Avenue, +353 1 679 8290, www.phoenixparkbikes.com).
For location, see the map above.

GETTING AROUND DUBLIN

You'll do most of Dublin on foot, though when you need public
transportation, you'll find it readily available and easy to use. And
Dublin is a great taxi town, with reasonable, metered cabs easy to
hail. With a little planning, sightseers can make excellent use of
a two-day hop-on, hop-off bus ticket to link the best sights (see

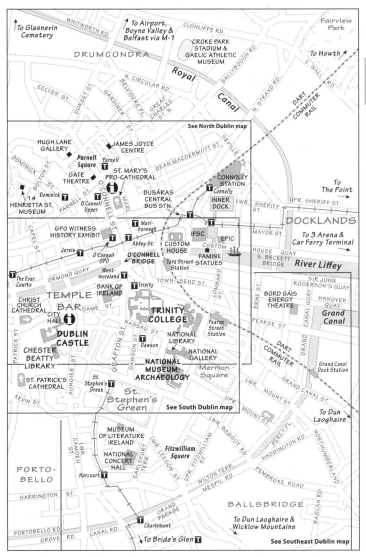

page 16). For cross-city travel, the LUAS tram system beats bus service for reliability and ease of transporting bags.

By Public Transportation

You can buy individual tickets for the bus, tram, and commuter train, or get a transit card that can be used on all three.

Transit Cards: The **Leap Card** is good for travel on Dublin's bus, DART, and LUAS routes, and fares are lower than buying individual tickets. Leap Cards are sold at TIs, newsstands, and mar-

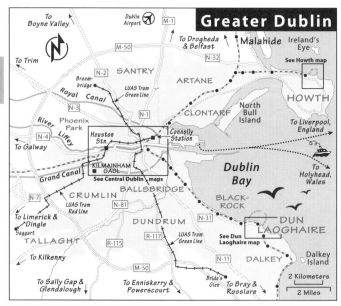

Greater Dublin

To Boyne Valley

Dublin Airport

M-1

To Trim

M-50

To Drogheda & Belfast

N-32

Malahide   Ireland's Eye

See Howth map

N-2   SANTRY

Broombridge

LUAS Tram Green Line

Royal Canal

ARTANE

N-3

N-1

CLONTARF

North Bull Island

HOWTH

River Liffey

Phoenix Park

Heuston Stn.

Connolly Station

To Liverpool, England

N-4

To Galway

KILMAINHAM GAOL

See Central Dublin maps

Grand Canal

BALLSBRIDGE

Dublin Bay

To Holyhead, Wales

N-7

CRUMLIN

LUAS Tram Red Line

N-81

BLACK-ROCK

To Limerick & Dingle

Saggart

DUNDRUM

N-31

DUN LAOGHAIRE

TALLAGHT

R-115

R-117

LUAS Tram Green Line

See Dun Laoghaire map

To Kilkenny

M-50

N-11

DALKEY

Dalkey Island

To Sally Gap & Glendalough

To Enniskerry & Powerscourt

Bride's Glen

To Bray & Rosslare

2 Kilometers

2 Miles

kets citywide—look for the leaping-frog logo—and can be topped up (€5 refundable deposit, www.leapcard.ie).

For those staying in Dun Laoghaire or Howth—or on a long-term stay in Dublin—the **Leap Visitor Card** may be a better option. It covers unlimited travel on Dublin's buses (including to and from the airport), DART, and LUAS trams (€8/1 day, €16/3 days, €32/7 days, each "day" equals 24 hours from first use, http://about. leapcard.ie/leap-visitor-card). Buy it at the airport or the Dublin Bus office (Upper O'Connell Street).

The **Do Dublin Freedom Card** includes a 72-hour Leap Visitor Card (see above) and the 48-hour Do Dublin hop-on, hop-off bus (described below, under "Tours in Dublin"). You can buy it in advance online, at the Do Dublin airport desk (Terminal 1), or at the Dublin Bus office, at their Upper O'Connell Street office or at their kiosk in the Stephen's Green Shopping Center (€45, +353 1 844 4265, www. dodublin.ie).

Buses: Public buses are cheap and cover the city thoroughly. Most lines start at the four quays (riverfront streets) that are nearest O'Connell Bridge. If you're away from the center, nearly any bus takes you back downtown. Some bus stops are "request only," so if you see your bus coming, flag it down. Tell the driver where you're going and they'll tell you the fare (€1.70-3, price depends on the number of stops; bring coins, as drivers don't make change). The Dublin Bus office has free route maps and sells transit cards (Mon-Fri 9:00-17:30, closed Sat-Sun, 59 Upper O'Connell Street, +353 1 873 4222, www.dublinbus.ie).

LUAS Trams: The city's street-tram system has two main lines, red and green. The **red line** is most useful for tourists, with an east-west section connecting the Heuston and Connolly train stations (a 20-minute ride apart) at opposite edges of the central zone. In between, the Busáras, Smithfield, and Museum stops are handy. Useful north-south **green line** stops are at St. Stephen's Green, Trinity College, and both ends of O'Connell Street. The lines don't intersect: The closest transfer point is a 100-yard walk between the red-line Abbey Street stop and the green-line General Post Office (GPO) stop on O'Connell Street. Monitors at boarding platforms display the time and end destination of the next tram; make sure you're on the right platform for the direction you want to go (€1.70 for Zone 1—which covers all the major sights, buy tickets at machine, 6/hour, runs until 24:45, www.luas.ie).

DART Commuter Trains: Speedy commuter trains run along the coast, connecting Dublin with suburban Dun Laoghaire (south) and Howth (north). Think of the DART line as a giant "C" that serves coastal suburbs from Bray in the south up to Howth (€2.65, €5 round-trip—valid same day only, fares may be a bit higher depending on destination, buy tickets at machine, 3-6/hour, +353 1 703 3504, www.irishrail.ie).

By Taxi or Uber

Taxis are everywhere and easy to hail on the streets. You can also ask your hotelier to order a taxi for you, or you can call one yourself with the Free Now app (easy to set up, works like Uber). Cab-

bies are generally honest, friendly, and good sources of information (figure about €9-14 for most in-city rides). While Uber is available in Dublin, you'll still get a taxi-certified driver and a metered rate, so it's more efficient to just hail one yourself or use the Free Now app.

Tours in Dublin

While Dublin's physical treasures are lackluster by European standards, the gritty city has a fine story to tell and people with a natural knack for telling it. It's a good town for walking tours, and competition is fierce. Pamphlets touting creative walks are posted all over town. Taking an evening walk is a great way to meet other travelers.

For help finding the departure points of the following recommended tours, see the map on page 42.

ON FOOT

∩ To sightsee on your own, download my free two-part Dublin City Walk audio tour. For **Trinity College campus tours,** worth ▲▲, see page 42.

Walking Tours

▲▲Historical Walking Tours of Dublin

This walk, led by history grads, is your best introduction to Dublin's basic historic strip (including Trinity College, Parliament House, Dublin Castle, Christ Church Cathedral, Grafton Street, and St. Stephen's Green). You'll get the story of the city, from its Viking origins to the present, including the roots of Ireland's struggle with Britain. You'll stand in front of buildings that aren't much to look at, but give your guide lots to talk about (May-Sept daily at 11:00

and 15:00, April and Oct daily at 11:00, Nov-March Fri-Sun at 11:00). Walks last just over two hours (€14, RS%—€2 off, ask when booking; if booking online, email to request discount, free for kids under 14, departs from front gate of Trinity College, private tours available, +353 87 688 9412, www.historicalinsights.ie, info@historicaltours.ie).

1916 Rebellion Walking Tour

This two-hour walk breathes gritty life into the most turbulent year in modern Irish history, when idealistic Irish rebels launched the Easter Rising—eventually leading to independence from Britain. Lorcan Collins (author, historian, and host of the *Revolutionary Ireland* podcast) and his guides are passionate about their subject (€15, RS%—€2 off, email to request discount; March-Oct Mon-Sat at 11:30, Sun at 13:00; Nov-Feb Sat-Sun only; departs from International Bar at 23 Wicklow Street, +353 86 858 3847, www.1916rising.com, Lorcan@1916rising.com).

Pat Liddy's Walking Tours

Pat Liddy, a top local historian, has a crew of guides who lead an assortment of informal 2-hour walks of Dublin. The "Highlights and Hidden Corners" tour is a good introductory route, covering O'Connell Street and the General Post Office building, then across the river through Temple Bar, by Christ Church Cathedral and the grounds of Dublin Castle, and ending near Trinity College (€20, RS%—€2 off, email to request discount; daily at 11:00 in peak season; Mon, Wed, Fri, and Sat only in off-season; meet in front of Dublin Bus office at 59 Upper O'Connell Street—see map on page 62, +353 1 832 9406, +353 87 905 2480, www.walkingtours. ie, info@walkingtours.ie). While it's smart to book ahead, you can just show up. Pat's guides are also available for private tours (€220/half-day).

Pub Crawls

▲▲Traditional Irish Musical Pub Crawl

This entertaining tour visits the upstairs rooms of three pubs. There, you'll listen to two musicians talk about, play, and sing traditional Irish music. While having only two musicians makes the music a bit thin (Irish music aficionados will say you're better off just finding a good session), the evening—though touristy—provides a real education in traditional Irish music. The musicians clearly enjoy introducing rookies to their art and are very good at it (and really funny). In the summer, this 2.5-hour tour frequently sells out, so book ahead online (€19, RS%—use code "RSIRISH" online, beer extra, Wed-Sat at 19:30 but schedule variable—check website, maximum 65 people, meet upstairs at Gogarty's Pub, 58 Fleet Street in Temple Bar, +353 1 475 8345, www. musicalpubcrawl.com). They also offer a dinner-show version with more music and Irish dancing (€55, starts at 17:30).

Dublin Literary Pub Crawl

Two actors take 40 or so tourists on a walk, stopping at four pubs, and with clever bantering *craic* (fun and conversation) introduce the language of James Joyce, Seán O'Casey, and W. B. Yeats. The two-hour tour is punctuated with 20-minute pub breaks (free time to drink and socialize). This is an easygoing excuse to drink beer

DUBLIN

Dublin at a Glance

▲▲▲Book of Kells in the Trinity Old Library An exquisite illuminated manuscript, Ireland's most important piece of art from the early Middle Ages. **Hours:** Mon-Sat 8:30-17:00, Sun from 9:30; Oct-April Mon-Sat 9:30-17:00, Sun 12:00-16:30. See page 40.

▲▲▲National Museum of Archaeology Excellent collection of Irish treasures from the Stone Age to today. **Hours:** Tue-Sat 10:00-17:00, Sun-Mon from 13:00. See page 44.

▲▲▲Kilmainham Gaol Historic jail used by the British as a political prison—today a museum that tells a moving story of the suffering of the Irish people. **Hours:** Guided tours daily 9:30-17:45, June-Aug until 18:15, Oct-March until 17:15. See page 69.

▲▲Historical Walking Tour of Dublin This group tour is your best introduction to Dublin. **Hours:** May-Sept daily at 11:00 and 15:00, April and Oct daily at 11:00, Nov-March Fri-Sun at 11:00. See page 12.

▲▲Traditional Irish Musical Pub Crawl A fascinating, practical, and enjoyable primer on traditional Irish music. **Hours:** Generally Wed-Sat at 19:30, but schedule variable. See page 13.

▲▲Trinity College Campus Tour Ireland's most famous school, best visited with a tour. **Hours:** Daily, first tour generally at 9:00 or 9:30, last tour generally at 16:30, no tours on Sun in off-season. See page 40.

▲▲Chester Beatty Library American expatriate's sumptuous collection of literary and religious treasures from Islam, Asia, and medieval Europe. **Hours:** Mon-Sat 9:45-17:30, Wed until 20:00, Sun from 12:00, closed Mon in winter. See page 54.

▲▲Temple Bar Dublin's rowdiest neighborhood, with shops, cafés, theaters, galleries, pubs, and restaurants—a great spot for live (but touristy) traditional music. See page 60.

▲▲O'Connell Street Dublin's grandest promenade and main drag, packed with history and ideal for a stroll. See page 34.

▲▲EPIC: The Irish Emigration Museum Creative displays about the Irish diaspora highlight the impact emigrants make on their new homelands. **Hours:** Daily 10:00-18:45. See page 61.

▲▲14 Henrietta Street A time capsule of urban Dublin life, following the 150-year decline of an aristocratic Georgian townhouse into tenement slum. **Hours:** Guided tours generally hourly Wed-Sun 10:00-16:00, closed Mon-Tue. See page 66.

▲National Gallery of Ireland Fine collection of top Irish painters and European masters. **Hours:** Sun-Mon 11:00-17:30, Tue-Sat 9:15-17:30, Thu until 20:30. See page 50.

▲**Museum of Literature Ireland (MoLI)** Exhibits and treasures exploring Ireland's literary heritage. **Hours:** Tue-Sun 10:30-18:00, closed Mon. See page 51.

▲**Dublin Castle** Once the city's historic 700-year-old castle, now a Georgian palace, featuring ornate English state apartments. **Hours:** Daily 9:45-17:45. See page 52.

▲**Christ Church Cathedral** Neo-Gothic cathedral on the site of an 11th-century Viking church. **Hours:** Mon-Sat 10:00-18:00, Sun 13:00-15:00 & 16:30-18:00. See page 58.

▲**Dublinia** A fun, kid-friendly look at Dublin's Viking and medieval past with a side order of archaeology and a cool town model. **Hours:** Daily 10:00-17:30. See page 59.

▲**St. Patrick's Cathedral** The holy site of legend where St. Patrick first baptized Irish converts. **Hours:** Mon-Fri 9:30-17:00, Sat-Sun 9:00-18:00 except during Sun services, shorter hours off-season. See page 60.

▲*Jeanie Johnston* **Tall Ship and Famine Museum** Floating exhibit on the River Liffey explaining the Famine period that prompted desperate transatlantic crossings (by tour only). **Hours:** Mon-Fri 10:00-16:30, Sat-Sun until 16:00, shorter hours off-season. See page 64.

▲**GPO Witness History Exhibit** Immersive presentation on the 1916 Easter Rising and its impact on Irish history, situated in the General Post Office building that served as rebel headquarters. **Hours:** Tue-Sat 10:00-17:00, closed Sun-Mon. See page 65.

▲**Guinness Storehouse** The home of Ireland's national beer, with a museum of beer-making, a gallery of clever ads, and Gravity Bar with panoramic city views. **Hours:** Mon-Thu 10:00-19:00, Fri-Sat 9:30-20:00, Sun 9:30-19:00, shorter hours off-season. See page 70.

▲**National Museum of Decorative Arts and History** Shows off Irish dress, furniture, silver, and weaponry with a special focus on the 1916 rebellion, fight for independence, and civil war. **Hours:** Tue-Sat 10:00-17:00, Sun-Mon from 13:00. See page 73.

▲**Gaelic Athletic Association Museum** High-tech museum of traditional Gaelic sports (hurling and Irish football). **Hours:** Mon-Sat 9:30-17:00, Sun from 10:00. May be closed on Sat-Sun if there's a game —check ahead. See page 73.

in busy pubs, meet other travelers, and get a dose of witty Irish lit (€16, daily at 19:30, Nov-March Thu-Sun only; reserve ahead in July-Aug when it can fill up, otherwise just show up; meet upstairs in the Duke Pub—off Grafton on Duke Street, +353 87 263 0270, www.dublinpubcrawl.com, info@dublinpubcrawl.com). Their once-a-week morning **Literary Walk** leads you on an insightful 1.5-hour stroll among the Dublin haunts of Irish wordsmiths (€15, Mondays at 10:30, must book in advance).

Food Tours
Fab Food Trails Dublin
For a 2.5-hour, six-stop edible education in Irish food, consider this food tour. With a small group (maximum 12 people), you'll visit a cheesemonger, try some fancy meats with wine, go to a bakery, hit the produce market, and maybe slurp an oyster, all with the good *craic* of your food-loving guide (€70, RS%—10 percent off with code "RSteves," April-Oct Thu-Sat at 10:00, Sat only in off-season, meeting point varies, +353 1 497 1245, fabfoodtrails.ie).

Local Guides
With so much fascinating history and such a rich tradition of storytelling, it's no wonder there are plenty of smart and entertaining Dublin historians who work as private guides and are eager to tailor a tour to your interests. In addition to these three, the guides at **Pat Liddy's Walking Tours** can be booked privately (see earlier).

Witty **Dara McCarthy** will proudly show you around his hometown—when he's not leading one of my Rick Steves' Ireland tours (€140/2.5 hours, +353 87 291 6798, dara@daramccarthy.com).

Suzanne Cole is good guide, both charming and smart (€140/2.5 hours, +353 87 225 1262, suza.cole@gmail.com).

Jack Walsh is a local actor who's both high-minded and soft-spoken (€180/half-day, +353 87 228 1570, walshjack135@gmail.com).

BY BUS
▲Hop-On, Hop-Off Bus Tours

Dublin works well for a hop-on, hop-off bus tour, which is an excellent way to orient yourself on arrival. Two companies with roofless double-deckers do similar 1.5-hour circuits of the city with about 25 stops. With running commentaries (either live or recorded), buses run frequently enough that you can use them for efficient sightseeing (stops include the far-flung Guinness Storehouse, Kilmainham Gaol, and Phoenix Park). Both companies let one kid ride free with each adult.

Do Dublin (green buses) drivers provide fun and quirky narration. Your ticket includes free entry into the Little Museum of Dublin and a free walking tour from Pat Liddy's Walking Tours—ask the driver (€27/24 hours, €32/48 hours, daily 9:00-17:00, until 19:00 in summer, 2/hour, booking office at 59 Upper O'Connell Street—see map on page 62, +353 1 703 3024, www.dodublin.ie).

Big Bus Tours (maroon-and-cream buses) has a handy "red route" that works well for sightseeing (€30/24 hours, €40/48 hours, cheaper online, daily 9:00-17:00, 3/hour, +353 87 427 8555, www.bigbustours.com). They also offer a one-hour panoramic night tour (€20, nightly at 19:00 and 20:30, leaves from 13 Upper O'Connell Street, halfway between the Spire and the Gresham Hotel—see map on page 62).

BY BIKE
Cycle Dublin Bike Tours
Pedal across this flat city on a fun 2.5-hour guided tour that covers points of interest and history on both sides of the river (€30, daily at 10:30, Fri-Sat also at 14:00, private tours available, meet at 2 Whitefriar Place, +353 86 252 6578, https://cycledublinbiketours.ie).

Lazy Bike Tour Company
For a less strenuous option, you can grab a bright orange e-bike and matching vest, and buzz along on a guided tour that covers sights from Dublin Castle to Kilmainham Gaol. Tours start in Temple Bar and last two hours (€40, daily at 10:00 and 14:00, book in advance in summer, meet at Drury Street Car Park (Bike Park), +353 1 443 3671, www.lazybiketours.com).

Dublin City Walk

This two-part self-guided walk covers the basic sights in the center of town on both sides of the River Liffey. It can be done as a light, fast-paced overview in about two hours. Or you can use it to lace together many of the city's top sights. It's long, but easy to do in two sections (south and north of the river).

Take this walk at the beginning of your Dublin visit to get the lay of the land—physically, culturally, and historically. As several of the stops and passageways along the route are closed after dark, this walk is best during normal business hours. (Doing it after-hours works, but you'll need to skip a few stops.)

For background on some of the historical events and person-alities introduced on this walk, refer to the "Modern Ireland's Turbulent Birth" sidebar, later.

🎧 Download my free two-part Dublin City Walk audio tour.

PART 1: SOUTH DUBLIN

• *Start at the southernmost end of Grafton Street, where the city's thriving pedestrian boulevard meets its most beloved park. Stand before the big arch.*

❶ St. Stephen's Green

This city park, worth ▲, was originally a medieval commons—a space for grazing livestock. The park got its start in 1664, when

the city leased some of the land as building lots, and each tenant was obligated to plant six trees.

Gradually the green was surrounded with fine Georgian buildings and access was limited to those affluent residents. ("Georgian" is British for Neoclassical, named for the period from 1714 to 1830 when four consecutive King Georges occupied the British throne.) Those were the glory days, when Dublin, both wealthy and powerful, was the number-two city in Britain, and squares and boulevards built in the Georgian style gave the city an air of grandeur. In 1880, the park was opened to the public, and today it provides a grassy refuge for all Dubliners.

The gateway before you is the **Fusiliers Arch.** It commemo-rates Irishmen who died fighting in the British Army in the Boer War (against Dutch settlers in South Africa from 1899-1902).

Under the curve of the arch, see the names of those who lost their lives. In Dublin's crush-ingly impoverished tenements of the time, one of the few ways for a young man without means to improve his lot would be to join the army (regular meals, proper clothing, and a chance to "see the world"). You can read a little of the Irish struggle into the names: Captains were Protestant elites with English names, and grunts were Catholic with Cath-olic names. Many more grunts died.

Two decades later, Ireland was em-broiled in its own battles against Britain, and sentiments had evolved. With Irishmen fighting to end centuries of English domination, locals considered the Fusiliers Arch to be a memorial to those who fought for Britain—and began referring to it as "Traitors Arch." A key Dublin battleground during the 1916 Easter Rising was in and around this park. Step around to the east side of the arch and look up to see **bullet marks** scarring the memorial.

During the short-lived Easter Rising revolt, a group of passionate Irish rebels—a mishmash of romantic poets, teachers, aristocratic ladies, and slum dwellers—dug trenches in the park, believing they were creating fortified positions. They hadn't figured on veteran British troops placing snipers atop the nearby Shelbourne Hotel (with a bird's-eye view into the trenches). The park is dotted with reminders of the long Irish struggle against the British, like the **memorial stone** honoring Irish rebel O'Donovan Rossa (a few steps into the park past the arch). An oration at his funeral in 1915 was a catalyst that helped galvanize the rebels who would rise in 1916.

Take a quick walk into the park, strolling a couple hundred yards around the lake counterclockwise. (Find a park map on a post to orient yourself.) Walk past the palm trees (imported from China, they are the only palm that can grow on the Emerald Isle).

As you round the lake, look for a rocky knoll in the trees. Hiding there, on a terrace that's popular for outdoor plays and weddings, is a monument to **W. B. Yeats** (by Henry Moore). Walking across the terrace and then down, you come to the **central garden,** packed at sunny lunchtimes with Dublin office workers. On a pleasant afternoon, this open space is a wonderful world apart from the big city. With romantic gazebos, duck-filled ponds, and relaxed people, today the park seems to celebrate Irish freedom.

From the central garden continue circling the **lake,** going over a bridge and back to the arch. The ducks you see are a traditional part of the scene. Generations of Dubliners treasure memories of coming here on Sundays as little kids to feed them. (Lately bully seagulls and pigeons are muscling into duck country.)

• *Exiting through the big arch, you're facing busy, pedestrianized Grafton Street (we'll go down it later). First we'll make a swing around the block to the right: Cross the street (watch for trams) and head right to the first corner, then go left, down Dawson Street.*

You can just make out the **Dawson Lounge** *(a.k.a. the "tiniest pub in Dublin," on the left at #25). Next door (#27), the* **Celtic Whiskey Shop** *is a reminder that in recent years Ireland has exported more whiskey than Scotland. To find out why, and maybe score a free sample, drop in. The big white Georgian building across the street is the...*

DUBLIN

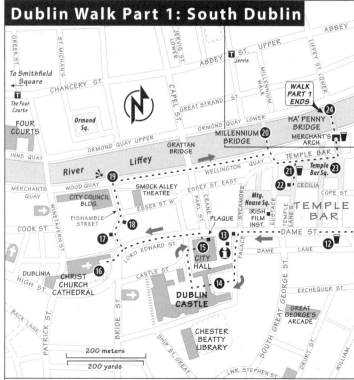

Dublin Walk Part 1: South Dublin

- ❶ St. Stephen's Green
- ❷ Mansion House
- ❸ Grafton Street
- ❹ Bewley's Oriental Café
- ❺ St. Teresa's Catholic Church
- ❻ Ulysses Plaque
- ❼ Trinity College's Old Library
- ❽ Trinity College
- ❾ Parliament House & a Grand Boulevard
- ❿ Irish House of Lords
- ⓫ Molly Malone Statue
- ⓬ The Bank Bar
- ⓭ Green Post Box
- ⓮ Dublin Castle
- ⓯ Dublin City Hall
- ⓰ Christ Church Cathedral
- ⓱ Viking Dublin
- ⓲ Handel's Hotel
- ⓳ River Liffey & View of the Four Courts
- ⓴ Millennium Bridge
- ㉑ Temple Bar
- ㉒ Wall of Fame & Irish Pop Music
- ㉓ Temple Bar Square
- ㉔ Ha'Penny Bridge

❷ Mansion House

Built in 1710, this is where Dublin's Lord Mayor lives. The building played roles in both of Ireland's wars.

In 1918 Ireland elected its representatives to the British Parliament—and chose mostly separatist members of the Sinn Féin ("Ourselves") party. The Sinn Féin parliamentarians refused to take their seats at Westminster in London. Instead, in January 1919,

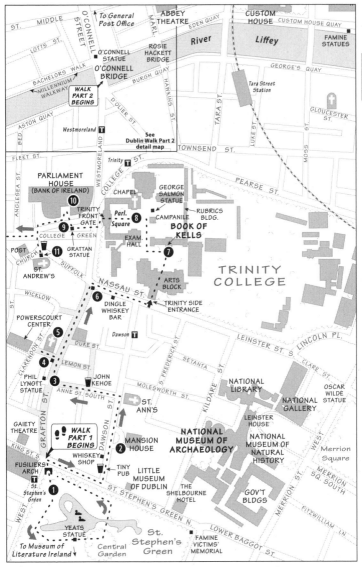

they created their own Irish Parliament (the Dáil Éireann) and met here, in an annex behind the Mansion House. The establishment of this rogue parliament in defiance of British rule kicked off the Irish War of Independence.

Three years later, they'd thrown off British rule, but found themselves at odds over the terms of the Anglo-Irish Treaty to end the war. Unable to agree, those opposed to ratification—led by Dáil Éireann president Éamon de Valera—marched out of parlia-

ment in protest. Within a few months, their festering disagreements ignited into the tragic Irish Civil War, eventually won by the pro-treaty forces of Michael Collins.

• *Continue down Dawson Street to the corner of Anne Street South. The large neo-Romanesque (late 19th century) church on the right is the Anglican **St. Ann's Church**, where Irish author Oscar Wilde was baptized and Bram Stoker (of Dracula fame) was married.*

*Turn left onto Anne Street South and walk two blocks toward Grafton Street, past a line of busy independent retailers and a popular pub, **John Kehoe**. Customers typically spill into the street with their*

beloved pints in hand. (Technically, it's illegal to drink on the street, but it's only selectively enforced.) This legacy pub is part of the Dublin landscape: Dubliners often refer to landmark pubs rather than street names when giving directions.

Stop and enjoy the scene when you reach the busy, pedestrian boulevard.

❸ Grafton Street

Grafton Street is Dublin's most desirable retail address. It was pedestrianized in 1983, much to the consternation of local retailers—who were soon pleased to discover that business improved without all the traffic. Ireland's Celtic Tiger economic boom (2000-2008) gave the country Europe's hottest economy and a thriving tech sector. Business was so good that retail rents skyrocketed, which drove away small shops. Today Grafton Street is filled with mostly international retailers and a surging torrent of shoppers.

We'll stroll the boulevard to the right in a moment. But first, go directly across Grafton to Harry Street: A half-block up you'll find a hairy rock star. This life-sized bronze statue with bass guitar, picks wedged behind the strings as fan tributes, is **Phil**

Lynott, Ireland's first hard-rock star. He lived a short, fast life and is remembered for his band Thin Lizzy (of "The Boys Are Back in Town" fame). You could build an entire Dublin walk around its many popular musicians and rock stars...but I won't.

DUBLIN

• *Return to Grafton Street, take a left, and join the river of pedestrians. Stop 50 yards down at the venerable café on the left...*

➍ Bewley's Oriental Café

Bewley's is a Dublin tradition that your Irish great-grandfather would remember for its well-priced comfort food. The facade is done in an ornate neo-Egyptian, Art Deco style (built after the excitement of the discovery of King Tut's tomb in 1922). Approach it as if visiting an art gallery filled with people eating. Walk to the very back of the ground floor (or go up to the balcony on the left) to view its famous stained-glass windows by artist Harry Clarke (1881-1931). For Clarke, famous for decorating churches with his exquisite windows, this is a rare secular commission, celebrating the four classical orders of column design. A fine Irish craftsman/artist, Clarke first learned his trade from his father, a stained-glass painter, and was part of the Irish Arts and Crafts movement. You're free to wander upstairs (if open) for more Bewley art. (For more about the restaurant, see page 89.)

• *A couple of steps farther down Grafton, turn left on the narrow lane called Johnson's Court. About 50 feet down, through the ornate archway, find a peaceful church.*

➎ St. Teresa's Catholic Church

Tucked away as if hiding, St. Teresa's was built in 1792—one of the first Catholic churches allowed in Ireland after the gradual relaxing of the Penal Laws passed by the Protestant parliament (1691-1760) to regulate Catholics.

For a century, Catholics and their clergy were forced to practice their religion secretly, celebrating Mass at hidden rural "Mass rock" altars. But by the 1790s, the British government felt secure enough to allow some

DUBLIN

Catholic churches to be built again. They also wanted to appease the Irish—who could have been getting ideas as they observed Catholic France beheading its monarchs. Catholics were allowed to worship in actual churches as long as they kept a low profile.

Daniel O'Connell (1775-1847), an enlightened member of parliament, campaigned for Catholic equality and held political meetings at St. Teresa's. He brought down the last of those Penal Laws in 1829 by championing the Catholic right to vote. (We'll learn more about O'Connell later on this walk.)

• *Now stroll down Grafton Street. As you make your way, take a moment to enjoy a local busker or chat at a street stall with a salt-of-the-earth woman selling flowers (these are mother-daughter hand-me-down businesses). Step out of the flow of humanity to glance up the side streets. Commercial as this street is, it has standards—notice that the arches are not golden at McDonald's. At the end of the pedestrianized section of Grafton Street, at the right corner, find a brass plaque in the pavement.*

❻ *Ulysses* Plaque

The little brass plaque on the ground, rubbed shiny by foot traffic, marks a spot mentioned in James Joyce's most famous novel, *Ulysses.* Passionate Irish-lit fans know Joyce's challenging, stream-of-consciousness work, which unfolds as a single day in the life of Leopold Bloom—June 16, 1904. The date is celebrated every year in Dublin as "Bloomsday," with scholars and enthusiasts dressing in period Edwardian garb and quoting passages from Joyce. This plaque is one of many *Ulysses* points of interest in town (there are even frequent public readings from the novel; see page 53).

• *Turn right and go a block on busy Nassau Street, passing the recommended* **Dingle Whiskey Bar** *(on the right, with 180 whiskeys on its shelves—an art form in itself). At the next corner, on the opposite (leafy) side of Nassau Street, is a side entrance to* **Trinity College.** *Follow the stream of students into the modern bunker-like Arts Building (note that on Sat-Sun after 18:00 the campus may be closed. In that case, refer to your map and walk left to the university's front door.)*

Walk through the hall, exit the building down the ramp, and survey the grassy courtyard. The grand, gray three-story building with a line of tourists is...

❼ Trinity College's Old Library

The college's Old Library houses the **Book of Kells,** a medieval masterpiece of calligraphy and illustration. The ground floor contains the actual 1,200-year-old book (containing the gospels of Matthew, Mark, Luke, and John); the top floor is a venerable world of varnished wooden shelves giving a dignified home to a precious collection of reference books and artifacts, including an original copy of the 1916 Proclamation of the Irish Republic, which an-

DUBLIN

nounced Ireland's dramatic split with Britain (for more on touring the library, see page 40).

• *Go around to the left of the Old Library to enter a larger and grander square. Walk to the center, where the smooth paths intersect, and face the* **Campanile** *(bell tower).*

❽ Trinity College

You're standing on Parliament Square, in the heart of Ireland's oldest seat of learning, founded in 1592 by Queen Elizabeth to set the ill-disciplined Irish on the straight and righteous path to Protestant learning. These cobblestones were trod by Trinity graduates like Jonathan Swift, Oscar Wilde, Bram Stoker, and Samuel Beckett. (You're surrounded by dorms and administration. The actual classrooms are mostly elsewhere.)

Behind the graceful Campanile are the red-brick **Rubrics,** the oldest remaining buildings on campus (c. 1712). Their facades sport a faintly Dutch look, due to their construction soon after the reign of Dutch-born King William III of Orange. He took the British throne jointly with his English wife/cousin Mary II, bringing Dutch architecture into vogue for a generation.

Fifty feet to the left of the Campanile is a white-marble statue of a seated man, grinning down on us from his pedestal. He's **George Salmon,** a mathematician, theologian, and provost in the late 1890s, who said women would enter Trinity over his dead body. Coincidentally, days after he died in 1904, the first women were admitted to Trinity College.

Trinity remains one of the world's great universities—and would be greater if not for the financial challenges of attracting top professors. Money raised by the hordes of tourists seeing the Book of Kells goes to support the cash-strapped university. And the college has put on a charm offensive to attract wealthy students from China, as the full tuition they pay subsidizes less-wealthy Irish students.

Now turn 180 degrees to face the front gate of the college. To your right and left stand two identically majestic buildings, each with four Corinthian columns. To your right is the college chapel, and to the left is the examination hall. During final exams, there tends to be a lot of student traffic between the two buildings, nick-named "heaven and hell."

• *Exit the campus through the front gatehouse, across hexagonal wooden pavers intended to dampen the sound of horse hooves. Before leaving the gatehouse, pretend you're a student—look at the posters to catch up on news, sports, rooms for rent, and plays and concerts.*

Exiting the college, you'll enter one of the most chaotic intersections in Dublin. Cross the street carefully to the traffic island at the bottom of the busy boulevard and stand before a statue of the guy who first cooked potatoes au Grattan (or an 18th-century member of the Irish House of Commons—you decide).

❾ Parliament House and a Grand Boulevard

The long street stretching straight in front of you is College Green, which becomes Dame Street, and then Lord Edward Street as it reaches Christ Church Cathedral, a half-mile away (and we're about to walk the entire thing). For simplicity, I'll just refer to it as "the boulevard."

Roughly 250 years ago, this spot marked the start of Dublin's version of a "Royal Mile," where the parliament, castle, university, and big banks all intersected in full glory. Logically, this spot in front of parliament was also where serious protests took place. "No taxation without representation" was a rebel rallying cry against Britain here as it was in our 13 colonies.

The grand building with a rounded colonnade is the **Parliament House** (now home to the Bank of Ireland). The Irish House

of Commons and House of Lords met here until the 1801 Act of Union abolished the Irish parliament, moving its members to Westminster in London. Thus began Dublin's slow, century-long decay, from important British hub to largely impoverished, tenement-ridden backwater.

• *The original House of Lords survives in the bank. Drop in to see it, if it's open.*

❿ Irish House of Lords

The Irish parliament building was built in 1733 on the same model as the Houses of Parliament in London. It was the first purpose-built bicameral parliament. The House of Commons was eventually gutted, but the smaller House of Lords survived unaltered. Inside are tapestries celebrating Protestant victories over the indigenous and Catholic Irish, busts of British kings and admirals, and a fireplace carved of Irish oak. A big ceremonial silver mace represented the authority of the British monarch; nothing that occurred in this chamber was valid without the monarch's symbolic presence. A painting shows the appearance of the once-adjacent but now-gone House of Commons.

• *Leaving the bank, walk a block up the boulevard and take your first left (cross over at Ulster Bank), onto Church Lane. Go one block to an old church with a statue out front of a buxom maiden pushing a cart of wicker baskets.*

⓫ Molly Malone Statue

You've probably heard Dublin's unofficial theme song "Molly Malone"—now let's meet the woman commemorated in the tune.

The area around the Molly Malone statue (from 1988) is a popular hangout for street musicians—and for tourists wanting a photo with the iconic gal of Irish sing-along fame. She pauses cooperatively "in Dublin's fair city, where the girls are so pretty," to offer you "cockles and mussels, alive, alive-o" from her cart. (Tour guides created some bogus legend about good luck or good sex...and now tourists dutifully line up to help shine her bosom.)

The church was **St. Andrew's,** once a place of worship frequented by nearby members of parliament. Enjoy its 19th-century neo-Gothic stonework. Now decommissioned, its future is as a high-end food court.

Across the street is **O'Neill's** pub, with a sloppy and noisy wonderland of cozy alcoves scattered over three floors. Just for fun, enter on the right and work your way through its labyrinthine interior, eventually exiting on the left. The O'Neill family has had a pub at this intersection for over 300 years and has benefited from its strategic location: It lies directly between the church and parliament, with the power brokers of the time being regular patrons.

• *Return to the main boulevard, turn left, and continue a few doors to a very fancy bank (on the left with a red sandstone facade, brass details, and showy banners) that's now a very fancy pub. Step just inside for a dazzling view.*

⓬ The Bank Bar

Built in 1894, The Bank Bar staggers visitors with its Victorian opulence. Back then, banks had to dazzle elite clients to assure them the bank was financially solid. Today, Dublin's banks have vacated such palaces for modern offices, and many ornate former bank interiors—like this one—now dazzle diners.

Even if you're not eating or drinking here, you're welcome to stand just inside the door for a look. The stained-glass ceiling still sparkles. The many mirrors make the space seem larger, and the ornate floor tiles and crow's nest balcony catch the eye. In a case by the door, a faithful replica of the Book of Kells is under glass. A stately painting of the Custom House (surrounded by the ships so vital to Dublin's economy) fills the wall on

the left. And on the right is a painting of Parliament House. The paintings face each other as pillars of society: commerce and governance. In the back-right corner are seven male busts: the seven patriot signers of the 1916 Proclamation of Irish Independence, martyrs for the Irish Republic—all executed at Kilmainham Gaol. (The basement restrooms are flanked by four old bank vaults.)

• *Exit the bar, turn left, and walk a couple of minutes (two long blocks) until you see a green post box (in front of the TI). Here's a fun fact while you walk: in Ireland, car license plates tell when and where a car was registered: 222-D indicates 2022, second half of the year, in Dublin.*

⓭ Green Post Box

An innocent-looking, round green postal box stands sentry in a small sidewalk plaza. Like all Irish post boxes, it's Irish green. But look closely at the elaborate monogram at knee height. It's an ornate "E" for "Edward," woven with "R" for "Rex" (Latin for "king")—indicating that this box dates from just before World War I, during the reign of King Edward VII (son of Victoria)—who reigned over Ireland as part of the United Kingdom of Great Britain and Ireland. Once royal red, after Ireland won its independence it was more practical to just paint the post poxes Irish green and call it good, rather than replace them. In 1922, this box, with its high-profile location at the entry to the grounds of Dublin Castle, was the first to be

painted green. If a Royalist were to scratch the paint to show some underlying red, it would be repainted green before you could say Guy Fawkes.

• *Ahead is City Hall. But first we'll take a short detour, looping left and then right through the courtyard of Dublin Castle before emerging just beyond City Hall.*

⓪ Dublin Castle

While Dublin Castle today shows only scant remains of its medieval architecture, it was the center of English power for 700 years, from its initial con-struction in 1204 (under bad King John of Magna Carta fame) until Britain handed the reins back to the Irish in 1922. Today, it's a prime example of a Georgian palace and the location for ceremonial af-fairs of state. The castle's  grand state rooms are open to the public (see page 52).

• *Leave the castle grounds through the gate at the top of the courtyard. On your right, facing the busy boulevard, is the stately City Hall, worth a visit to see its interior.*

⑮ Dublin City Hall

Dublin's impressive City Hall, worth ▲, started life in 1779 as the Royal Exchange, where Irish and British currencies were ex-changed and where mer-chants gathered to dis-cuss trading affairs. It's a splendid example of the Georgian style then very popular in Britain.

It became City Hall in 1852 and was the site of the first fatalities of the 1916 Easter Rising, when  Irish rebels occupied it to control the main gate to Dublin Castle. Step inside (it's free) to feel the prosperity and confidence of Dub-lin in her glory days. The dramatic main-floor rotunda—with its grand Caesar-like statue of the great orator Daniel O'Connell (the city's first Catholic mayor, 1841)—was inspired by the Pantheon in Rome. (They get more rain here so the oculus—the opening in the ceiling—is covered.) A cycle of heroic paintings tells the city's history in a rare example of Arts and Crafts artwork from 1919. It was here, under the rotunda, that the body of Irish rebel leader Michael Collins lay in state after his assassination in 1922. On the floor, a Latin inscription translates to "Obedient citizens make a happy city."

• *Leave City Hall through the Dame Street exit, and take the stairs on your right. Halfway down, look on the wall for a* **bronze plaque** *establishing the British Imperial system of inches, feet, and yards (and miles)—which, thanks to our colonial heritage, the United States is saddled with. Find the Paris Metre—Ireland now uses the metric system.*

Now, we'll turn left on Dame Street and continue uphill on the big boulevard to the church tower in the distance. Enter the churchyard and walk past the downtrodden person sleeping on the bench. But wait...are those nail holes in his feet? It's a statue called **Homeless Jesus** *by the Canadian artist Timothy Schmalz.*

⓰ Christ Church Cathedral

The cathedral in front of you, worth ▲, is one of the oldest places of worship in Dublin. What you see today is an extensively renovated neo-Gothic structure dating from the 1870s, but its underground crypt goes back to 1172. An even earlier Viking-era church stood here back in the 1030s. Just beyond the *Homeless Jesus* statue, an excavation contains the low-lying ruins of a small 12th-century church building. The stones you see on the exterior of the southern transept (above the excavation site) are 12th-century Romanesque—one of the few original features not disturbed by later restorations (for more on the church, see page 58).

• *Leave the churchyard as you entered, turn left, and walk a few steps down Fishamble Street to the blocky concrete sign reading* Dublin City Council. *At your feet in the pavement is a marker celebrating some ancient history.*

⓱ Viking Dublin

You're standing on the site of Dublin's first Viking settlement, established in the mid-ninth century, with Fishamble Street as its fish market. When the foundations for the huge bunker-like modern offices of the Dublin City Council were dug in 1978, an intact Viking settlement was exposed. A treasure trove of artifacts was uncovered, carefully excavated, and catalogued by eager archaeologists. More than a million objects were found (the best are in the National Museum of Archaeology). Even so,

researchers were allowed only a short time to dig before the office building that stands here was erected, effectively burying the rest of the settlement under the pavement. Public protests were vehement and vocal, but to no avail. In an ironic twist, Dublin's citizens must come here to get planning permission to build. Sidewalk plaques (there are 18 scattered around) based on photos from the dig remind all who pass of what was found—and lost.

• *Walk farther downhill, passing* **Darkey Kelly's,** *a recommended pub with music nightly. At the end of the block, you'll see...*

⑱ Handel's Hotel

This hotel is named for the composer of the *Messiah* (with its beloved "Hallelujah Chorus"). The first public performance of this iconic oratorio took place in 1742 in a nearby music hall. Peek through the gate to the left of the hotel to see the remains of a surviving theater wall and a statue—a naked and fit Handel stands like a pillar saint atop organ pipes. Every year, on the April 13 anniversary of that premiere, this humble street fills with a full orchestra and 120 choral singers to perform the *Messiah* for the public.

• *Continue walking down Fishamble all the way to the river.*

⑲ River Liffey and View of the Four Courts

Look left. Across the river in the distance is a grand building with a green domed roof. This is the **Four Courts,** finished in 1802 and housing Ireland's Supreme Court. It was once the archive for irreplaceable birth and land records. When the Irish Civil War broke out in 1922, Irish nationalists opposed to British dominion occupied the building. Forces supporting the 1921 Anglo-Irish Treaty—led by Michael Collins—were left no alternative but to root them out with British-supplied artillery (the first shots of that tragic brother-against-brother conflict). The artillery onslaught resulted in the accidental detonation of rebel ammo in the Four Courts, sparking an intense fire that destroyed seven centuries of genealogical and historical records.

• *Turn right and walk downstream to the second bridge, the pedestrian-only Millennium Bridge. Walk halfway out to survey the scene.*

⑳ Millennium Bridge

From here the Liffey flows three miles to empty into the Irish Sea. Bordered on both sides by quays (the old English word for "wharf"), today the river is empty of vessels and contained by its concrete embankments. But it was once wider, with muddy banks, wooden piers, and sailing ships. After Vikings sailed their longboats down the Liffey in the ninth century, they built a ship harbor here, and for centuries afterward, the riverfront was the pumping heart of Dublin's commerce. The Liffey is a salty river, with high and low tides. Before the 1600s, boats could come this far upriver to the medieval port area. But with more bridges and bigger ships, the port moved farther and farther downstream. Today it's at the mouth of the river, three miles away.

Look downstream at the next bridge, the pedestrian-only **Ha' Penny Bridge,** a Dublin landmark since 1816. Its graceful cast-iron arch is a celebration of the emerging bridge engineering made possible by the Industrial Revolution. It's officially the "Wellington Bridge," named for Arthur Wellesley, the first duke of Wellington, who was born in Ireland, beat Napoleon at Waterloo, and became a British prime minister. (When teased

in Westminster about his Irish birth, he famously said, "Just because you're born in a stable doesn't make you a donkey.") It got its nickname because people paid half a penny ("Ha' penny") to cross the bridge rather than ride a ferry across the river—the only other option in the early 1800s.

We'll cross that bridge when we get to it. But first, let's head to the Temple Bar district, which stretches along the south bank of the river from here past the Ha' Penny Bridge.

• *Go a block inland from the river. At East Essex Street (and the Norsemen Pub), wander left into the heart of Dublin's infamous party district, known as...*

㉑ Temple Bar

Inspired by thriving bohemian cultural centers such as Paris' Left Bank and New York City's Greenwich Village, in 1991 Dublin scuttled a plan to demolish this neighborhood (filled with drugs, prostitutes, and decay) to build a bus station. Instead, the city imported quaint cobbles, gave tax breaks to entertainment businesses, and created a raucous party zone. The resulting tourist crowds and inflated beer prices drove away the locals long ago. (For more on Temple Bar, see pages 79 and 92.)

On the first corner slouches a pub called **The Temple Bar.** While it looks venerable, it's only 25 years old, built to cash in on the district's rising popularity as a night spot. It encapsulates the commercialism of the tourists' Temple Bar. Venture in and sample the scene.

You wouldn't know it by looking at Temple Bar, but since 2001 consumption of alcohol is down almost 20 percent in Ireland. In 2018, Guinness launched its first nonalcoholic beer—perhaps thinking young people don't have as much time for hangovers. Starbucks-like coffee shops are everywhere. A North Dublin pub called The Virgin Mary serves no booze. While Irish pubs are in vogue around the world, here on the Emerald Isle a thousand pubs have closed in the last decade.

• *From The Temple Bar pub, side-trip right a block, up Temple Lane South, and stop at the corner of Cecilia Street.*

㉒ Wall of Fame and Irish Pop Music

The windows of the three-story, red "Wall of Fame" on your right are filled with photos of contemporary Irish musicians (Bob Geldof, Phil Lynott, Sinead O'Connor, U2, The Cranberries, and others). It

marks the location of the **Irish Rock 'n' Roll Museum**—worth a visit for rock fans interested in seeing studio space and vintage mixing boards used by famous acts (visit by €16.50 guided tour only, drop in or check their website for tour times, www.irishrocknrollmuseum.com).

Behind you, above the now-closed Claddagh Records, the modest third floor once held studios where U2 did some of its earliest recording.

• *Return to the main street and turn right into...*

㉓ Temple Bar Square

This square is the geographic heart of the Temple Bar district and a favorite haunt of street musicians. The quaint-looking pubs that front it are re-creations built in the early 2000s, when the area became so popular that pubs could sell the most expensive pints in town. Stand here on a Saturday night and you'll see how this party zone got its reputation for rowdy noise and drunken antics.

• *Walk along the square, then turn left up the narrow lane called Merchant's Arch, toward the river and* ㉔ *Ha' Penny Bridge. Walk to the midway point of the bridge and celebrate the end of your South Dublin walk.*

You are very near the starting point of the second half of this walk, which will take us up O'Connell Street. To get there, continue across the river, turn right, and walk to the O'Connell Bridge via the wooden riverside Millennial Walkway.

DUBLIN

PART 2: O'CONNELL STREET AND IRISH HEROES

This part of our Dublin walk features a series of sights and monuments recalling Ireland's long fight for independence. It's a straight line through the heart of North Dublin from the O'Connell Bridge up O'Connell Street to the Garden of Remembrance, a memorial park dedicated to the "terrible beauty" of this freedom-loving island.

❶ O'Connell Bridge

This bridge—actually wider than it is long—spans the River Liffey, which historically has divided the wealthy, cultivated south side of town from the working-class north side.

While there's plenty of culture on the north bank, even today the suburbs (a couple of miles north of the Liffey) are considered rougher and less safe. Dubliners joke that "north siders" are known as "the accused," while "south siders" are addressed as "your honor."

From the bridge, look downstream. Modern Dublin is developing before you. During the Celtic Tiger boom, the Irish subsidized and revitalized this formerly dreary quarter. While the "Tiger" died with the great recession of 2008-2009, Dublin's economy is booming again—as illustrated by the forest of cranes marking building sites in the east end of town and the massive redevelopment of Upper O'Connell Street (which you'll see later on this walk).

❷ O'Connell Street and Historic Highlights

Turn and look up the broad and grand O'Connell Street, leading from the O'Connell Bridge through the heart of north Dublin.

Since the 1740s, the street has been a 45-yard-wide promenade, and once the first O'Connell Bridge connected it to the Trinity College side of town in 1794, it became Dublin's main drag. It's named after Daniel O'Connell, Dublin's first Catholic mayor—we'll meet him in a moment.

These days, the city has made the street (worth ▲▲) more pedestrian-friendly, and a tram line runs alongside the median. Though filled with touristy fast-food joints and souvenir shops, O'Connell Street echoes with history. The median is dotted with statues remembering great figures

Dublin Walk Part 2:
O'Connell Street & Irish Heroes

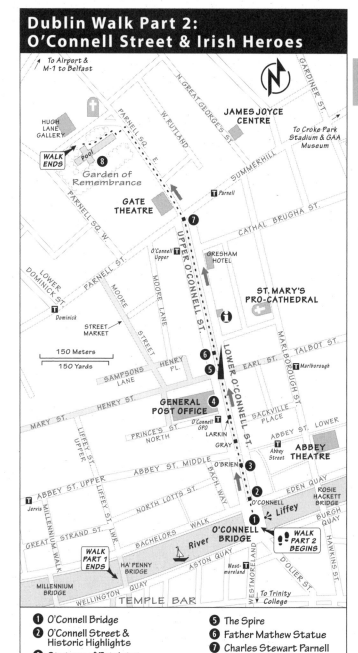

To Airport &
M-1 to Belfast

N. GREAT GEORGE'S ST.

GARDINER ST.

HUGH LANE GALLERY

PARNELL SQ. N.

W. RUTLAND

JAMES JOYCE CENTRE

To Croke Park Stadium & GAA Museum

WALK ENDS

Pool

8

Garden of Remembrance

SUMMERHILL

T Parnell

GATE THEATRE

PARNELL SQ. E.

CATHAL BRUGHA ST.

7

PARNELL SQ. W.

UPPER O'CONNELL ST.

O'Connell Upper

GRESHAM HOTEL

ST. MARY'S PRO-CATHEDRAL

LOWER DOMINICK ST.

PARNELL ST.

MOORE ST.

MOORE LANE

T Dominick

STREET MARKET

150 Meters

150 Yards

SAMPSONS LANE

HENRY PL.

6

5

LOWER O'CONNELL ST.

EARL ST.

T Marlborough

MARLBOROUGH ST.

TALBOT ST.

HENRY ST.

MARY ST.

GENERAL POST OFFICE

4

SACKVILLE PLACE

PRINCE'S NORTH

O'Connell GPO T

LARKIN

GRAY

ABBEY ST. LOWER

T Abbey Street

ABBEY THEATRE

LIFFEY ST. UPPER

ABBEY ST. UPPER

ABBEY ST. MIDDLE

O'BRIEN

3

BACH. WAY

NORTH LOTTS ST.

T Jervis

MILLENNIUM WALK

2

O'CONNELL

EDEN QUAY

ROSIE HACKETT BRIDGE

Liffey

BURGH QUAY

GREAT STRAND ST. LWR.

BACHELORS WALK

River

1

O'CONNELL BRIDGE

WALK PART 2 BEGINS

HAWKINS ST.

WALK PART 1 ENDS

HA' PENNY BRIDGE

ASTON QUAY

West-moreland T

WESTMORELAND ST.

D'OLIER ST.

MILLENNIUM BRIDGE

WELLINGTON QUAY

TEMPLE BAR

To Trinity College

1 O'Connell Bridge

2 O'Connell Street & Historic Highlights

3 Statues of Patriots

4 General Post Office & GPO Witness History Exhibit

5 The Spire

6 Father Mathew Statue

7 Charles Stewart Parnell Monument

8 Garden of Remembrance

from Ireland's past—particularly the century (1830-1930) when Ireland rediscovered its roots and won its independence.

• *Now head north up O'Connell Street, walking on the wide, tree-lined median strip toward the spike in the sky. Along the way, you'll see statues honoring great Irishmen (starting with the man for whom the street is named).*

❸ Statues of Patriots

Daniel O'Connell (1775-1847) was known as The Liberator for founding the Catholic Association, a political group that demand-ed Irish Catholic rights in the British Par-liament. Having personally witnessed the violence of the French Revolution in 1789, O'Connell chose peaceful, legal means to achieve his ends. A charismatic speaker, he organized thousands of nonviolent protes-tors into "monster meetings," whose sheer size intimidated the British authorities. O'Connell went on to become the first Cath-olic mayor of Dublin (1841-1842). Below his statue (commissioned in 1880), Lady Ire-land, chains broken around her feet, points to the great emancipator (holding articles of emancipation). The many bullet holes date from the 1916 Easter Rising.

William Smith O'Brien (1803-1864), the next statue up the street, was O'Connell's contemporary and the leader of the nation-alist Young Ireland Movement. He was more willing to use force to achieve Irish self-determination. After a failed uprising in Tip-perary, he was imprisoned and sentenced to death in 1848, but then exiled to Australia.

Sir John Gray (1816-1875) was one of Daniel O'Connell's strongest supporters and advocated for the repeal of union with Britain. He was also re-sponsible for bringing safe drinking water to Dublin, overcoming cholera and other wa-terborne diseases that had plagued the city.

James Larkin (1876-1947), arms out-stretched, was the founder of the Irish Transport and General Workers Union. His attempts to relieve tenement poverty through more humane work conditions earned him love from the downtrodden and enmity from the one percent of his day. The general strike he called in 1913 is considered by many to be the first shot in the War of Independence.

Larkin was arrested on this spot for trying to make a speech during the seven-month Dublin Lockout. A protest over that arrest degenerated into a riot, police brutality, and several fatalities.

• *On your left is the...*

❹ General Post Office (GPO)

This is not just any post office. It was from here that the nationalist activist Patrick Pearse read the Proclamation of Irish Inde-
pendence in 1916, kicking off the Easter Rising. On Easter Monday 1916, the building itself became the rebel headquarters and the scene of a bloody five-day siege—a kind of Irish Alamo. The post office was particularly strategic because it housed the tele-

graph nerve center for the entire country. Its pillars are still pock-marked with bullet holes. On the right as you enter, the engaging **GPO Witness History** exhibit brings the dramatic history of this important building to life (for details, see page 65).

• *At the intersection of O'Connell and Henry streets, marvel up at...*

❺ The Spire

There used to be a tall column at this intersection, crowned by a statue of the British hero of Trafalgar, Admiral Horatio Nelson. It
was blown up in 1966—the IRA's contribution to the local celebration of the Easter Rising's 50th anniversary. The spot is now occupied by a sculpture called the Spire: 398 feet of stainless steel. While it trumpets rejuvenation on its side of the river, it's a memorial to nothing and has no real meaning. Dubliners call it the tallest waste of €5 million in all of Europe. Its nickname? Take your pick: the Stiletto in the Ghetto, the Stiffy on the Liffey, the Pole in the Hole, or the Poker near the Croker (after nearby Croke Park).

The "erection at the intersection" was built for the millennium, but Dublin was only able to get it up in 2004. Before leaving, have fun standing close and looking way up.

• *A few steps farther along is a statue of...*

❻ Father Mathew

A leader of the temperance movement of the 1830s, Father Theobald Mathew was responsible, some historians claim, for enough Irish peasants staying sober to enable Daniel O'Connell to organize them into a political force. By 1844, over half the adult population of Ireland had signed his total abstinence pledge. Then the onset of the Great Potato Famine diffused his efforts and sent thousands to their graves or onto emigration ships. Desperation drove Ireland back to whiskey.

• *Over the next few years, the district ahead on the left will undergo a massive revitalization (if funding holds up). The fancy* **Gresham Hotel** *(on the right), a good place for an elegant tea or beer, recalls travel to Dublin in the gilded Victorian age. Standing boldly at the top of O'Connell Street is the...*

❼ Charles Stewart Parnell Monument

Ringing the monument are the names of the four ancient provinces of Ireland and all 32 Irish counties (north and south, since this was erected before Irish partition). The monument honors Charles Stewart Parnell (1846-1891), the member of parliament who nearly won Home Rule for Ireland in the 1880s (and who served time at Kilmainham Gaol for his nationalist activities). A Cambridge-educated Protestant of landed-gentry stock, Parnell envisioned a modern, free Irish nation of Catholics as a secular democracy. The Irish people, who remembered their grandparents' harsh evictions during the Great Potato Famine, came to love Parnell (despite his privileged birth) for his tireless work to secure fair rents and land tenure. Momentum seemed to be on his side. With the British prime minister of the time, William Gladstone, favoring a similar form of Home Rule, it looked as if Ireland was on its way toward independence as a Commonwealth nation, similar to Canada or Australia.

Then a scandal broke around Parnell and his mistress, the wife of another parliament member. The press—egged on by powerful Catholic bishops (who didn't want a secular, free Irish state)—battered away at the scandal until finally Parnell was driven from office. Wracked with exhaustion and only in his mid-40s, Parnell died brokenhearted. (Sex scandals have a persistent way of shaping history.)

After that, Ireland became mired in the conflicts of the 20th century: an awkward independence (1921) featuring a divided island, a bloody civil war, and sectarian violence for decades afterward. Now, for over 20 years, peace has prevailed on this troubled isle.

• *Continue uphill, straight up Parnell Square East. At the* **Gate Theatre** *(on the left), actors Orson Welles, Geraldine Fitzgerald, and James Mason had their professional stage debuts. One block up, on the left, is the...*

❽ Garden of Remembrance

Honoring the victims of the 1916 Easter Rising, this memorial garden marks the spot where the rebel leaders were held before

being transferred to Kilmainham Gaol. The park was dedicated in 1966 on the 50th anniversary of the revolt that ultimately led to Irish independence. The bottom of the cross-shaped pool is a mosaic of Celtic weapons, symbolic of how the early Irish

proclaimed peace by breaking their weapons and throwing them into a lake or river. In the statue (beyond the pool, under the flag), four siblings morph into swans, referring to the Children of Lir of Irish mythology. W. B. Yeats' poem "Easter, 1916" describes the transformation—"a terrible beauty is born"—as independent Ireland enters a new, if uncertain, age. The Irish flag flies above: green for Catholics, orange for Protestants, and white for the hope that they can live together in peace.

One of modern Ireland's most stirring moments occurred here in May 2011, when Queen Elizabeth II made this the first stop on her historic visit to the Republic—the first by a reigning British monarch in 100 years. She laid a wreath at the statue under the Irish flag and bowed her head in silence out of respect for the Irish rebels who had fought and died trying to gain freedom from her United Kingdom. This was a hugely cathartic moment for both nations.

• *Your walk is over. To get back to the center, just hop on your skateboard—it's downhill all the way to the river (or grab any tram from the Parnell Street stop—they all go to Trinity College).*

DUBLIN

Sights in Dublin

For information on Dublin's City Hall as well as additional detail on many of the sights described below, see "Dublin City Walk," earlier, or ∩ download my free audio tour.

SOUTH OF THE RIVER LIFFEY
Trinity College

Founded in 1592 by Queen Elizabeth I to establish a Protestant way of thinking about God, Trinity has long been Ireland's most prestigious college. Originally, the student body was limited to rich Protestant men. Women were admitted in 1903, and Catholics—though allowed entrance to the school much earlier—were given formal permission by the Catholic Church to study at Trinity in the 1970s (before that they risked mortal sin). Today, more than half of Trinity's 18,000 students are women, and there are Catholic, Jewish, and Muslim student societies on campus. Notice that on campus, the official blue-and-white signs are bilingual—and the Irish comes first.

There are two worthwhile experiences here: a tour of the campus and the Book of Kells exhibit in the library.

▲▲Trinity College Campus Tour

Guided 45-minute tours provide an overview of the many and varied departments at the college, take you to little-known corners of the campus, and give you a peek at student life past and present.

Tours can be booked in conjunction with a visit to the Book of Kells, which is where the campus tour ends.

Cost and Hours: €15-tour only, €27-includes Book of Kells entry, book online in advance; tours run daily, first tour generally at 9:00 or 9:30, last tour generally at 16:30, no tours on Sun in off-season; www.tcd.ie/visitors/book-of-kells.

▲▲▲Book of Kells in the Trinity Old Library

The Book of Kells—a 1,200-year-old manuscript of the four gospels—was elaborately inked and meticulously illustrated by faithful monks. Combining Christian symbols and pagan styles, it's a snapshot of medieval Ireland in transition. Arguably the finest piece of art from the Middle Ages, the Book of Kells shows that monastic life in this far fringe of Europe was far from dark.

Cost and Hours: €16, €27 includes Trinity campus tour (described above), buy timed-entry ticket online in advance (or risk not getting in); Mon-Sat 8:30-17:00, Sun from 9:30; Oct-April Mon-

Sat 9:30-17:00, Sun 12:00-16:30; download helpful self-guided audio tour to your phone before your visit (bring earbuds), +353 1 896 2320, www.tcd.ie/visitors/book-of-kells.

Background: The Book of Kells was a labor of love created by dedicated Irish monks cloistered on the remote Scottish island of Iona. They slaughtered 185 calves, soaked the skins in lime, scraped off the hair, and dried the skins into a cream-colored writing surface called vellum. Only then could the tonsured monks pick up their swan-quill pens and get to work.

The project may have been underway in 806 when Vikings savagely pillaged and burned Iona, killing 68 monks. The survivors fled to the Abbey of Kells (near Dublin). Scholars debate exactly where the book was produced: It could have been made entirely at Iona or at Kells, or started in Iona and finished at Kells.

For eight centuries, the glorious gospel sat regally atop the high altar of the church at Kells, where the priest would read from it during special Masses. In 1654, as Cromwell's puritanical rule settled in, the book was smuggled to Dublin for safety. Here at Trinity College, it was first displayed to the public in the mid-1800s. In 1953, the book got its current covers and was bound into four separate volumes.

Visiting the Book of Kells: Your visit has three stages: 1) an exhibit on the making of the Book of Kells, including poster-sized reproductions of its pages (your best look at the book's detail); 2) the Treasury, a darkened room containing the Book of Kells itself and other, less ornate contemporaneous volumes; and, upstairs, 3) the Old Library (called the Long Room), containing a precious collection of 16th- to 18th-century books and historical objects.

The Exhibit: The Turning Darkness into Light exhibit, with a one-way route, puts the illuminated manuscript in its historical and cultural context. This is important as it prepares you to see the original book and other precious manuscripts in the treasury. Make a point to spend some time in this exhibit before reaching the actual Book of Kells.

Look for the two continuously running video clips that show the ancient art of bookbinding and the exacting care that went into transcribing the monk-uscripts. They vividly depict the skill and patience needed for the monks' work.

The Book: The Book of Kells contains the four gospels of the Bible (two are on display at any given time). Altogether, the manuscript is 680 pages long (or 340 "folios," the equivalent of one sheet, front and back). The Latin

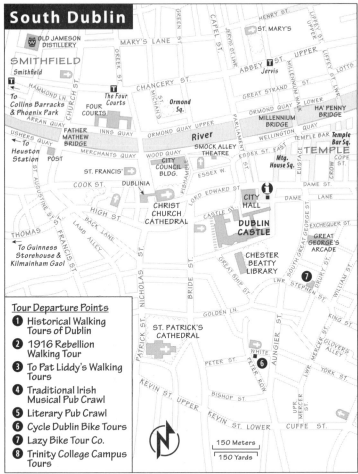

South Dublin

Tour Departure Points
1 Historical Walking Tours of Dublin
2 1916 Rebellion Walking Tour
3 To Pat Liddy's Walking Tours
4 Traditional Irish Musical Pub Crawl
5 Literary Pub Crawl
6 Cycle Dublin Bike Tours
7 Lazy Bike Tour Co.
8 Trinity College Campus Tours

150 Meters
150 Yards

calligraphy—all in capital letters—follows ruled lines, forming neat horizontal bars across the page. Sentences end with a "period" of three dots.

The text is elaborately decorated—of the hundreds of pages, only two are without illustration. Each gospel begins with a full-page depiction of an Evangelist and his symbol: Matthew (angel), Mark (lion), Luke (ox), and John (eagle). The apostles pose stiffly, like Byzantine-style icons, with almond-shaped eyes and symmetrically creased robes. Squint at the amazing detail. The true beauty lies in the intricate designs that surround the figures.

The colorful book employs blue, purple, red, pink, green, and yellow pigments—but no gold leaf. Letters and borders are braided together. On most pages, the initial letters are big and flowery, like in a children's fairy-tale book.

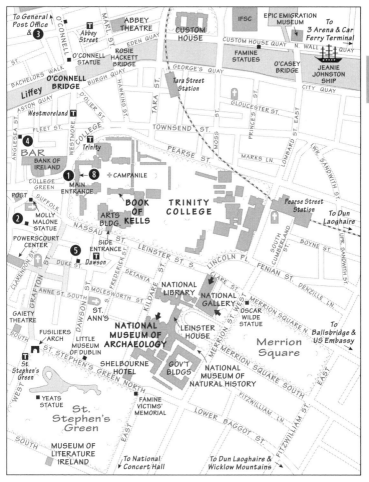

DUBLIN

Notice how the playful monks might cross a "t" with a fish, form an "h" from a spindly-legged man, or make an "e" out of a coiled snake. Animals crouch between sentences. It's a jungle of intricate designs, inhabited by tiny creatures both real and fanciful.

Scholars think three main artists created the book: the "goldsmith" (who did the filigree-style designs), the "illustrator" (who specialized in animals and grotesques), and the "portrait painter" (who did the Evangelists and Mary).

The Old Library: The Long Room, the 200-foot-long main chamber of the Old Library (from 1732), is stacked to its towering ceiling with 200,000 books. Lining the room are about 40 marble busts of famous writers, philosophers, and scholars (Shakespeare,

Plato, Jonathan Swift). For centuries, the busts represented only men—until 2022, when four women were added.

Among the displays here, you'll find one of a dozen surviving original copies of the **1916 Proclamation of the Irish Republic.** Patrick Pearse read out its words at Dublin's General Post Office on April 24, 1916, starting the Easter Rising that led to Irish independence. Notice the inclusive opening phrase ("Irishmen and Irishwomen") and the seven signatories (each of whom was later executed).

Another national icon is nearby: the oldest surviving **Irish harp,** from the 15th century (while often called the Brian Boru harp, it was crafted 400 years after the death of this Irish king). The brass pins on its oak and willow frame once held 29 strings. In Celtic days, poets—highly influential with kings and druid priests—wandered the land, uniting the people with songs and stories. The harp's inspirational effect on Gaelic culture was so strong that Queen Elizabeth I (1558-1603) ordered Irish harpists to be hung and their instruments smashed. Even today, the love of music here is so intense that Ireland is the only country with a musical instrument as its national symbol. You'll see this harp's likeness on the back of Irish euro coins, on government documents, and on every pint of Guinness.

▲▲▲National Museum of Archaeology

Showing off the treasures of Ireland from the Stone Age to modern times, this branch of the National Museum is itself a national treasure. The soggy marshes and peat bogs of Ireland have proven perfect for preserving old objects. You'll see 4,000-year-old gold jewelry, 2,000-year-old bog mummies, 1,000-year-old Viking swords, and the collection's superstar—the exquisitely wrought Tara Brooch. Visit here to get an introduction to the rest of Ireland's historic attractions: You'll find a reconstructed passage tomb like the one at Newgrange, Celtic art like the Book of Kells, Viking objects from Dublin, a model of the Hill of Tara, and a sacred cross from the Cong Abbey. Hit the highlights of my tour, then browse the exhibits at will, all well described throughout.

Cost and Hours: Free, Tue-Sat 10:00-17:00, Sun-Mon from 13:00, between Trinity College and St. Stephen's Green on Kildare Street, +353 1 677 7444, www.museum.ie.

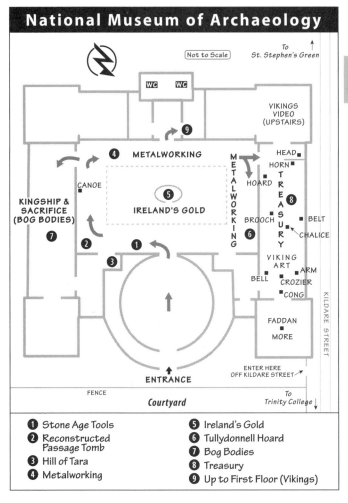

National Museum of Archaeology

DUBLIN

Not to Scale

To St. Stephen's Green

WC **WC**

VIKINGS VIDEO (UPSTAIRS)

❹ **METALWORKING**

HEAD

HORN

CANOE

HOARD

M E T A L W O R K I N G

T R E A S U R Y ❽

KINGSHIP & SACRIFICE (BOG BODIES) ❼

❺ **IRELAND'S GOLD**

BROOCH

BELT

CHALICE

❷

❶

❻

VIKING ART

BELL

ARM

CROZIER

CONG

❸

FADDAN MORE

KILDARE STREET

↑ **ENTRANCE**

ENTER HERE OFF KILDARE STREET

FENCE

Courtyard

To Trinity College

❶ Stone Age Tools	❺ Ireland's Gold
❷ Reconstructed Passage Tomb	❻ Tullydonnell Hoard
❸ Hill of Tara	❼ Bog Bodies
❹ Metalworking	❽ Treasury
	❾ Up to First Floor (Vikings)

➔ Self-Guided Tour

• *Follow this tour with the help of this book's map. On the ground floor, enter the main hall and get oriented: In the center (down four steps) are displays of prehistoric gold jewelry. To the left are the bog bodies, to the right is the Treasury room, and upstairs is the Viking world. Let's start at the very beginning.*

❶ **Stone Age Tools:** Glass cases hold flint and stone ax-heads and arrowheads (7,000 BC). Ireland's first inhabitants—hunters and fishers who came from Scotland—used these tools. These early people also left behind standing stones (dolmens) and passage tombs.

❷ **Reconstructed Passage Tomb:** At the corner of the room, you'll see a typical tomb circa 3,000 BC—a mound-shaped, heavy stone structure, covered with smaller rocks, with a passage leading into a central burial chamber where the deceased's ashes were interred. The vast passage tombs at Newgrange and Knowth are similar but many times bigger.

• *In the smaller room to the left of the passage tomb is a gallery devoted to the...*

❸ **Hill of Tara:** The famous passage-tomb burial site at Tara, known as the Mound of the Hostages, was used for more than 1,500 years as a place to inter human remains. The cases in this side gallery display some of the many exceptional Neolithic and Bronze Age finds uncovered at the site.

Over the millennia, the mound became the very symbol of Irish heritage. This is where Ireland's kings claimed their power, where St. Patrick preached his deal-clinching sermon, and where, in 1843, Daniel O'Connell rallied Irish patriots to demand their independence from Britain (see illustration in the small poster on the left wall).

• *Back in the big room, walk along the length of a 50-foot-long dugout canoe, from centuries before Christ and pickled in a bog. Then turn right.*

❹ **The Evolution of Metalworking:** Around 2500 BC, Ireland discovered how to make metal—mining ore, smelting it in furnaces, and casting or hammering it into shapes. The rest is prehistory. You'll travel through the Bronze Age (ax-heads from 2000 BC) and Iron Age (500 BC) as you examine assorted spears, shields, swords, and war horns. The cauldrons made for everyday cooking were also used ceremonially to prepare elaborate ritual feasts for friends and symbolic offerings for the gods.

• *The most impressive metal objects are four steps down in the center of the hall. Visit the square room at the lowest level.*

❺ **Ireland's Gold:** Ireland had only modest gold deposits, mainly gathered by prehistoric people panning for small nuggets and dust in the rivers. But the jewelry they left, some of it more than 4,000 years old, is exquisite. The earliest fashion choice was a broad necklace hammered flat (a *lunula*, so called for its crescent-moon shape). This might be worn with accompanying earrings and sun-disc brooches. The **Gleninsheen Collar** (c. 700 BC) was found in 1932 by a farmer in one of the characteristic limestone crevices of the Burren region of County Clare. It's thought that this valuable status symbol was hidden there during a time of conflict, then forgotten (or its owner killed); an offering to a pagan god would

more likely have been left in a body of water (the portal to the underworld).

Later Bronze Age **jewelry** was cast from clay molds into bracelets and unique "dress fasteners" that you'd slip into button-holes to secure a cloak. Some of these gold objects may have been gifts to fertility gods, offered by burying them in marshy bogs.

DUBLIN

• *Back up the stairs, in the corner near the main entry, find the* ❻ *Tul-lydonnell Hoard, discovered in Donegal in 2018. The four heavy gold rings, from about 1000 BC, weigh about two pounds each and are very plain. They likely were just a way to store one's wealth in the days before someone thought of coins and banks.*

Return to the long dugout canoe to enter the Kinship & Sacrifice room containing...

❼ **Bog Bodies:** When the Celts arrived in Ireland (c. 500 BC-AD 500), they brought with them a mysterious practice: They brutally murdered sacrificial slaves or prisoners and buried them in bogs. Four bodies (each in its own tiny theater with a description outside)—shriveled and leathery, but remarkably preserved—have been dug up from around the Celtic world.

Clonycavan Man is from Ireland. One summer day around 200 BC, this twenty-something man was hacked to death with an ax and disemboweled. In his time, he stood 5'9" and had a Mohawk-style haircut, poofed up with pine-resin hair product im-ported from France. Today you can still see traces of his hair. Only his upper body survived; the lower part may have been lost in the threshing machine that unearthed him in 2003.

Why were these people killed? It appears to have been a form of ritual human sacrifice of high-status people. Some may have been enemy chiefs or political rivals. The sacrifices could have been offerings to the gods to ensure rich harvests and good luck. Other items (now on display) were buried along with them—gold brace-lets, royal cloaks, finely wrought cauldrons, and leather garments.

• *Head across the main room again to enter the...*

❽ **Treasury:** Irish metalworking is legendary, and this room holds 1,500 years of exquisite treasures. Working from one end of the long room to the other, you'll journey from the world of the pagan Celts to the coming of Christianity, explore the stylistic im-pact of the Viking invasions (9th-12th century), and consider the resurgence of ecclesiastical metalworking (11th-12th century).

Pagan Era Art: The carved stone head of a mysterious pagan god greets you (#19, circa AD 100). The god's three faces express the different aspects of his stony personality. This abstract style—typical of Celtic art—would be at home in a modern art museum. A bronze horn (#17, first century BC) is the kind of curved war trumpet that Celts blasted to freak out the Roman legions on the Continent (the Romans never invaded Ireland). The fine objects of the Broighter Hoard (#15, first century BC) include a king's golden collar decorated in textbook Celtic style, with interlaced vines inhabited by stylized faces. The tiny boat was an offering to the sea god. The coconut-shell-shaped bowl symbolized a cauldron. By custom, the cauldron held food as a constant offering to Danu, the Celtic mother goddess, whose mythical palace was at Brú na Bóinne.

Early Christian Objects: Christianity officially entered Ireland in the fifth century (when St. Patrick converted the pagan king), but Celtic legends and art continued well into the Christian era. You'll see various crosses, portable shrines (reliquaries) containing holy relics, and chalices decorated with Celtic motifs. The Belt Shrine (#32)—a circular metal casing that held a saint's leather belt—was thought to have magical properties. When placed around someone's waist, it could heal the wearer or force him or her to tell the truth.

The Ardagh Chalice (#30) and the nearby Silver Paten (#31) were used during Communion to hold blessed wine and bread. Get close to admire the elaborate workmanship. The main bowl of the chalice is gilded bronze, with a contrasting band of intricately patterned gold filigree. It's studded with colorful glass, amber, and enamels. Mirrors below the display case show that even the underside of the chalice was decorated. When the priest grabbed the chalice by its two handles and tipped it to his lips, the base could be admired by God.

Tara Brooch: A wealthy eighth-century Celtic man fastened his cloak at the shoulder with this elaborate ring-shaped brooch (#29), its seven-inch stickpin tilted rakishly upward. Made of cast and gilded silver, it's ornamented with fine, exquisitely filigreed gold panels and studded with amber, enamel, and colored glass. The motifs include Celtic spirals, snakes, and stylized faces, but the symbolism is neither overtly pagan nor Christian—it's art for art's sake. Despite its name, the brooch probably has no connection to the Hill of Tara. In display cases nearby, you'll see other similar (but less impressive) brooches from the same period—some iron, some bronze, and one in pure gold. In the designs of this elaborate metalwork you can see the Celtic aesthetics that inspired the illuminations of the Book of Kells.

Viking Art Styles: Vikings invaded Dublin around AD 840. As Vikings did, they raped and pillaged. But they also opened Ireland to a vast and cosmopolitan trading empire, from which they imported hordes of silver. Viking influence shows up in the decorative style of reliquaries like the Lismore Crozier (#43, in the shape of a bishop's ceremonial shepherd's crook) and the Shrine of St. Lachtin's Arm (raised in an Irish-power salute). The impressive Bell of St. Patrick (#24) was supposedly owned by Ireland's patron saint. After his death, it was encased within a beautifully worked shrine (displayed above) and kept safe by a single family, who passed it down from generation to generation for 800 years.

Cross of Cong: "By this cross is covered the cross on which the Creator of the world suffered." Running along the sides of the cross (#44), a Latin inscription tells us that it once held a sacred relic, a tiny splinter of the True Cross on which Jesus was crucified. That piece of wood (now lost) had been given in 1123 to the Irish high king, who commissioned this reliquary to preserve the splinter (it would have been placed right in the center, visible through the large piece of rock crystal). Every Christmas and Easter, the cross was fitted onto a staff and paraded through the abbey at Cong, then placed on the altar for High Mass. The extraordinarily detailed decoration

features gold filigree interspersed with colored glass, enamel, and (now missing) precious stones. Though fully Christian, the cross has Celtic-style filigree patterning and Viking-style animal heads (notice how they grip the cross in their jaws).

Before leaving the Treasury, enter the room behind the Cross of Cong and check out the **Faddan More Psalter**—a (pretty beat-up) manuscript of the Book of Psalms from the same era as the Book of Kells.

• *Now head up to the first floor to the Viking world. Start in the long hall directly above the Treasury, with the informative 25-minute video on the Viking influence on Irish culture.*

❾ **Viking Ireland** (c. 800-1150): Dublin was born as a Viking town. Sometime in the ninth century, Scandinavian warriors rowed their longships up the River Liffey and made camp on the south bank, around the location of today's Dublin Castle and Christ Church Cathedral. Over the next two centuries, they built "Dubh linn" ("black pool" in Irish) into an important trading post, slave market, metalworking center, and the first true city in Ireland. (See a model of Dublin showing a recently excavated area near Kilmainham Gaol.)

The state-of-the-art Viking boats worked equally well in the open ocean and shallow rivers, and were perfect for stealth invasions and far-ranging trading. Soon, provincial Dublin was connected with the wider world—Scotland, England, northern Europe, even Asia. The museum's displays of swords and spears make it clear that, yes, the Vikings were fierce warriors. But you'll also see that they were respected merchants (standardized weights and coins), herders and craftsmen (leather shoes and bags), fashion conscious (bone combs and jewelry), fun loving (board games), and literate (runic alphabet). What you won't see are horned helmets, which, despite the stereotype, are not Viking. By 1050, the pagan Vikings had intermarried with the locals, become Christian, and were melting into Irish society.

• *With time and interest, you could explore the...*

Rest of the Museum: You'll find exhibits dedicated to medieval Ireland, with items from daily life (ploughs, cauldrons), trade (coins, pottery), and religion (crucifixes and saints). The Egyptian room has coffins, *shabtis,* and canopic jars—but no mummies.

Other Museums South of Trinity College

Adjacent to the archaeology branch are these other major museums. Also nearby is **Leinster House.** Once the Duke of Leinster's home, it now hosts the Irish Dáil (parliament) and Seanad (senate).

▲National Gallery of Ireland

While not as extensive as the National Gallery in London, the collections here are well worth your time. The museum boasts an impressive range of works by European masters and displays the works of top Irish painters, including Jack B. Yeats (brother of the famous poet).

Cost and Hours: Free, fee for special exhibits, Sun-Mon 11:00-17:30, Tue-Sat 9:15-17:30, Thu until 20:30, Merrion Square West, +353 1 661 5133, www.nationalgallery.ie.

Tours: Take advantage of the free audio descriptions of select paintings in the gallery (stream them on your phone, bring earbuds). There are also free 45-minute guided tours (usually Sat-Sun—check online or at main information desk for times).

Visiting the Museum: There are two entrances—from Clare Street (modern entry into the Millennium Wing, where the shop and café are), and the original Merrion Square entrance, where we'll start. From this entry, you'll walk through a series of ground-floor rooms devoted to Irish painting. Perhaps the most iconic Irish work you'll see is the huge, melodramatic depiction of the *Marriage of Strongbow and Aiofe* by Daniel Maclise (c. 1854, in the gallery to the left as you enter the museum). It captures the chaotic union of Norman and Irish interests that signaled the start of English domination of Ireland 850 years ago. Notice how the defeated Irish writhe and lament in the bright light of the foreground, while the scheming Norman warlords skulk in the dimly lit middle ground. The ruins of conquered Waterford smolder at the back.

Visit the National Portrait Collection on the mezzanine level for an insight into the great personalities of Ireland. European masterworks are on the top floor, including a rare Vermeer (one of only 30-some known works by the Dutch artist) and a classic Caravaggio (master of chiaroscuro and dramatic lighting). In the modern Millennium wing, you'll find a Monet riverscape and an early Cubist Picasso still life.

National Museum of Natural History

Nicknamed "the dead zoo" by Dubliners, this cramped collection of stuffed exotic animals comes across like the locker room on Noah's Ark. But if you're into beaks, bones, bugs, and boars, this Victorian relic is for you. Standing tall above a sea of taxidermy, the regal skeleton of a giant Irish elk from the last Ice Age dwarfs a modern moose.

Cost and Hours: May be closed for renovation—check ahead. Free, Tue-Sat 10:00-17:00, Sun-Mon from 13:00, Merrion Square West, +353 1 677 7444, www.museum.ie.

National Library of Ireland

Literature holds a lofty place in the Irish psyche. To feel the pulse of Ireland's most influential poet, visit the W. B. Yeats exhibit in the library basement. The artifacts flesh out the very human passions of this poet and playwright, with samples of his handwritten manuscripts and surprisingly interesting mini documentaries of the times he lived in. (To access the rest of the library, including the reading rooms and family history research room, you need to apply for a membership, a.k.a. a Reader's Ticket).

Cost and Hours: Free, exhibit open daily 9:30-17:00, Tue-Wed until 19:00, +353 1 603 0200, 2 Kildare Street, www.nli.ie.

▲Museum of Literature Ireland (MoLI)

Facing St. Stephen's Green, the Museum of Literature Ireland (MoLI) highlights the country's illustrious literary past and present. Exhibits inhabit three levels of a 1765 Georgian building, once the home of the Catholic University of Ireland (the predecessor to University College Dublin). Displays explain the history of the house and university, explore the state of Irish writing during the early part of the 20th century (a particularly complex time in Irish history), celebrate famous local writers, and introduce contemporary writers. At one stop, you can listen to works narrated in Irish. The museum also delves into the world of James Joyce, including a model of Dublin marking spots featured in his books, a selection of his handwritten notebooks, and the first published copy of *Ulysses*.

Cost and Hours: €10, Tue-Sun 10:30-18:00, closed Mon, last entry one hour before closing, guided tour-€12 (includes entry fee, daily at 13:00), gardens, café, 86 St. Stephen's Green, +353 1 716 5900, https://moli.ie.

Merrion Square and Nearby
Merrion Square

Laid out in 1762, this square just east of the National Gallery is ringed by elegant Georgian houses decorated with fine doors—a Dublin trademark. (If you're inspired by the ornate knobs and knockers, there's a shop on nearby Nassau Street.) The park, once the exclusive domain of the residents (among them, Daniel O'Connell at #58 and W. B. Yeats at #82), is now a delightful public escape and ideal for a picnic. Oscar Wilde, lounging wittily on a boulder in the northwest corner (nearest the town center) and surrounded by his clever quotes, provides a fun photo op (see photo, next page).

Little Museum of Dublin

Facing St. Stephen's Green, this pint-sized museum, just five rooms in a Georgian mansion from 1776, is a creative labor of love focusing on recent Irish history and pop culture. Volunteers have covered its walls with historic bits and pieces of Dublin history—all donated by locals.

Cost and Hours: €10 includes 30-minute tour, daily 10:00-17:00, tours depart every 30 minutes, last tour at 16:00, 15 St. Stephen's Green, +353 1 661 1000, www.littlemuseum.ie.

Visiting the Museum: Your visit includes an entertaining 30-minute talk through two rooms covering 20th-century Dublin history. You can explore the rest of the museum on your own, with exhibits on Georgian Dublin, Irish rock 'n' roll (great for U2 fans), and a rotating exhibit. Memorabilia ranges from historic letters written by Irish nationalists Éamon de Valera and Michael Collins to mementos of John F. Kennedy's 1963 Dublin visit and Muhammad Ali's 1972 fight against Al Lewis in Croke Park.

Dublin Castle and Nearby
▲Dublin Castle

Built on the spot of the first Viking fortress, this castle was the seat of English rule in Ireland for 700 years. Located where the Poddle and Liffey rivers flowed together, making a black pool (*dubh linn* in Irish), Dublin Castle was the official residence of the viceroy who implemented the will of British royalty. What you see today is the stately Georgian

Dublin's Literary Life

Dublin in the 1700s, grown rich from a lucrative cloth trade, was one of Europe's most cultured and sophisticated cities.

The buildings were decorated in the Georgian style still visible today, and the city's Protestant elite shuttled between here and London, bridging the Anglo-Irish cultural gap. Jonathan Swift was the era's greatest Anglo-Irish writer—a brilliant satirist and author of *Gulliver's Travels* (1726). He was also dean of St. Patrick's Cathedral (1713-1745) and one of the city's eminent citizens.

Around the turn of the 20th century, Dublin produced some of the world's great modern writers. Bram Stoker was the creator of *Dracula.* Oscar Wilde penned *The Picture of Dorian Gray* and a clutch of fine plays. George Bernard Shaw wrote *Pygmalion, Major Barbara, Man and Superman,* and a host of other dramas. William Butler Yeats was a prolific poet and playwright of Irish themes. And James Joyce whipped up a masterpiece called *Ulysses.*

To dip your toe into the occasionally unfathomable depths of classic Irish lit, drop by the tiny Sweny's Pharmacy for one of its readings from *Ulysses* or other works by Joyce. This shrine for devotees of Joyce is a time capsule, looking just as the writer described it in his novel more than a hundred years ago. The text is passed around for all to read a section aloud. Even if you don't understand its obscure local references, appreciate the rhythm of its stream-of-consciousness verbal flow... and buy a bar of lemon soap on your way out (check schedule at www.sweny.ie, sometimes read in other languages, 1 Lincoln Place between Trinity College and Merrion Square).

version, built in the late 17th and 18th centuries on top of the old medieval castle (little of which can still be recognized beyond one remaining round turret). In this stirring setting, the Brits handed power over to Michael Collins and the Irish in 1922, as stipulated by the Anglo-Irish Treaty. Today, the castle is used for fancy state dinners, charity functions, and presidential inaugurations.

Cost and Hours: Visiting the courtyard is free, €12 for one-hour guided tour, €8 to visit on your own (state apartments only); daily 9:45-17:45; tours-about 8/day, first and last tours generally at 10:00 and 16:00; sporadically closed for private events, tickets sold in courtyard under portico opposite clock tower, +353 1 645 8813, www.dublincastle.ie.

Visiting the Castle: Standing in the courtyard, you can imagine the ugliness of the British-Irish situation. Notice the statue of justice above the gate—pointedly without her blindfold and admiring her sword. As Dubliners say, "There she stands, above her station, with her face to the palace and her arse to the nation."

If visiting on your own, you can walk through the lavish state apartments of this most English of Irish palaces. With a tour, you also get a look at the Chapel Royal and the medieval undercroft, where you'll see the foundations of the old English tower (from 1204, original Viking defenses, and the best remaining chunk of the 13th-century town wall).

▲▲Chester Beatty Library

This library—located in the gardens of Dublin Castle (worth a stroll in nice weather)—is an exquisite, delightfully displayed collection of rare ancient manuscripts and beautifully illustrated books from around the world, plus a few odd curios. These treasures were bequeathed by Alfred Chester Beatty (1875-1968), a rich American mining magnate who traveled widely, collected 66,000 objects assiduously, and retired in Ireland.

Cost and Hours: Free; Mon-Sat 9:45-17:30, Wed until 20:00, Sun from 12:00, closed Mon in winter; download free audioguide app to your phone; free one-hour guided tours on Wed, Sat, and Sun—must prebook online; recommended Silk Road Café, lockers, +353 1 407 0750, www.cbl.ie.

Visiting the Museum: The museum is on three floors, with the café and shop on the **ground floor.** Before exploring, watch the 10-minute film about Beatty. Then head upstairs to see the treasures he left to his adopted country.

I've described the exhibits starting two floors up, on the second floor. Note that exhibits rotate, so some of the items I mention may not be on display.

Sacred Traditions Gallery (Second Floor): This space is dedicated to sacred texts, illuminated manuscripts, and miniature paintings from around the world. The doors swing open, and you're greeted by a video highlighting a diverse array of religious rites—a Christian wedding, Muslims kneeling for prayer, whirling dervishes, and so on. The left side of the gallery is dedicated to Christianity; in the center is Islam; and to the right is East Asian religions.

Christianity: In the 1930s, Beatty acquired 1,800-year-old **Bible fragments and manuscripts,** which had recently been unearthed in Egypt. The Indiana Jones-like discovery of these Old and New Testament texts instantly bumped scholars' knowledge of the early Bible up a notch. Written in Greek on papyrus more than a century before previously known documents, these are some of the oldest versions of these texts in existence. Unlike most early Christian texts, the manuscripts were not rolled up in a scroll but bound in a book form called a "codex." On display you may see pages from a third-century Gospel of Luke or the Gospel of John (c. AD 150-200). Jesus died around AD 33, and his words weren't recorded until decades later. Most early manuscripts date from the fourth century, so these pages are about as close to the source as you can get.

Among the rarest of the discoveries were the **Letters (Epistles) of Paul.** The Beatty has a near-complete collection (112 pages) of Saint Paul's letters (AD 180-200), though only a few are on display. Paul, a Roman citizen (c. AD 5-67), was the apostle most responsible for spreading Christianity beyond Palestine. Originally, Paul reviled Christians. But after a mystical experience, he went on to travel the known world, preaching the Good News in sophisticated Athens and the greatest city in the world, Rome, where he died a martyr to the cause. Along the way, he kept in touch with Christian congregations in cities like Corinth, Ephesus, and Rome with these letters.

Other items you may see include gloriously illustrated medieval Bibles and prayer books, such as an intricate, colorful, gold-speckled **Book of Hours** (1408).

Islam: Muslims believe that the angel Gabriel visited Muhammad (c. 570-632), instructing him to write down his heavenly visions in a book—the Quran. You'll see Qurans with elaborate calligraphy and other sacred Islamic texts, some of which are beautifully illustrated. Find the rare illuminated manuscript of the **biography of Muhammad** (c. 1595), produced in Istanbul for an Ottoman sultan.

East Asian Religions: Various statues of Buddha, along with Chinese and Japanese Buddhist scrolls, attest to the pervasive influence of this wise man. Buddha was born in India, but his philosophy spread to China, Japan, and Tibet (see the mandalas). You'll also see writings from India, the land of a million gods and the cradle of Buddhism, Hinduism, Sikhism, and Jainism.

Arts of the Book (First Floor): The focus here is on the many forms a "book" can take—from the earliest clay tablets and papyrus scrolls, to parchment scrolls and bound codices, to medieval monks' wondrous illustrations, to the advent of printing and bookbinding. To the left is a section on Europe; the center is dedicated to Islam; and the Far East is covered in the area to the right.

Europe: Start with the cases on **Egyptian and other ancient writings.** Here, a hieroglyph-covered papyrus scroll from the Book of the Dead (c. 300 BC) depicts a pharaoh on his throne (left) presiding over a soul's judgment in the afterlife. The jackal-headed god Anubis (center-right) holds a scale, weighing the heart of a dead woman to see if it's light enough for her to level up to the next phase of eternity. Another case shows off small cuneiform tablets

Modern Ireland's Turbulent Birth

Imagine if our American patriot ancestors had fought both our Revolutionary War and our Civil War back to back—over a span of seven chaotic years—and then appreciate the remarkable resilience of the Irish people. Here's a summary of what happened when.

Easter Rising, 1916: A nationalist militia called the Volunteers (led by **Patrick Pearse**) and the socialist Irish Citizen Army (led by **James Connolly**) join forces in the Easter Rising, a week-long rebellion against British rule that is quickly defeated. The uprising is unpopular with most Irish, who are unhappy with the destruction in Dublin and preoccupied with the "Great War" on the Continent. But when 16 rebel leaders (including Pearse and Connolly) are executed, Irish public opinion reverses as sympathy grows for the martyrs and the cause of Irish independence.

Two important rebel leaders escape execution. Brooklyn-born **Éamon de Valera** is spared because of his American passport (the British don't want to anger a potential WWI ally). **Michael Collins,** a low-ranking rebel officer who fought in the Rising at the General Post Office, is sent to prison, where he refines urban guerrilla strategies. After his release, he blossoms as the rebels' military and intelligence leader in the power vacuum that followed the executions.

General Election, 1918: World War I ends and a general election is held in Ireland (the first in which women can vote). Promising to withdraw from the British Parliament and declare an Irish republic, the nationalist **Sinn Féin** party wins 73 out of 79 seats. Only 4 of 32 counties vote to maintain the Union with Britain (all 4 lie in today's Northern Ireland). Rather than take their seats in London, Sinn Féin representatives abstain from participating in a government they see as a foreign occupier.

War of Independence, 1919: On January 19, the abstaining Sinn Féin members set up a rebel government in Dublin called Dáil Éireann. On the same day, the first shots of the Irish War of Inde-

and cylinder seals from as far back as 2,500 BC. These objects from ancient Mesopotamia are older than the pyramids and represent the very birth of writing.

This section also includes displays illustrating the evolution of bookbinding and printing. The collection shows off some of the earliest surviving bindings, as well as the wide array of bindings through the centuries. The printing press with movable type was pendence are fired as rebels begin ambushing police barracks, which are seen as an extension of British rule. De Valera is elected by the Dáil to lead the rebels, with Collins as his deputy. Collins' web of spies infiltrates British intelligence at Dublin Castle. The Volunteers rename themselves the **Irish Republican Army;** meanwhile the British beef up their military presence in Ireland by sending in tough WWI vets, the Black and Tans. A bloody and very personal war ensues.

Anglo-Irish Treaty, 1921: Having endured the slaughter of World War I, the British tire of the extended bloodshed in Ireland and begin negotiations with the rebels. De Valera leads rebel negotiations, but then entrusts them to Collins (a clever politician, De Valera sees that whoever signs a treaty will be blamed for its compromises). Understanding the tricky position he's in, Collins signs the Anglo-Irish Treaty in December 1921, lamenting that in doing so he has signed his "own death warrant."

The Dáil narrowly ratifies the treaty, which ends the war and allows for the establishment of an independent dominion, the Irish Free State. But Collins' followers are unable to convince De Valera's supporters that the treaty's compromises are a stepping-stone to later full independence. De Valera and his anti-treaty disciples resign in protest. **Arthur Griffith,** founder of Sinn Féin, assumes the presidential post.

Irish Civil War, 1922-1923: In June 1922, the anti-treaty forces, holed up in the Four Courts building in Dublin, are fired upon by Collins and his pro-treaty forces—thus igniting the Irish Civil War. The British want the treaty to stand and even supply Collins with cannons, meanwhile threatening to reenter Ireland if the anti-treaty forces aren't put down.

In August 1922, Griffith dies of stress-induced illness, and Collins is assassinated 10 days later. Nevertheless, the pro-treaty forces prevail, as they are backed by popular opinion and better (British-supplied) military equipment. By April 1923, the remaining IRA forces dump (or stash) their arms, ending the civil war... but many bitter IRA vets vow to carry on the fight. De Valera distances himself from the IRA and becomes the dominant Irish political leader for the next 40 years.

perfected by Johannes Gutenberg in Germany around 1450. The printed sheets were folded, sewn together, and wrapped in a cover. With the engraving process, beautiful illustrations could also be reproduced on a mass scale. Until the 20th century, it was common for a book buyer to acquire the printed sheets and then select a lavish custom-made cover. Beatty had a special interest in northern European prints, especially the work of German **Albrecht Dürer,** one of the earliest artists to use printing (both woodcut and engraving) to tell a story. The library usually displays several Dürer prints.

Islamic World: Books and folios from the rich Persian culture include many secular texts, such as scientific texts and poetry. Some are richly illustrated and have elaborate calligraphy (in Arabic, Persian, or Turkish).

Imperial works from Ottoman Turkey and paintings from 17th-century Mughal India show how later Muslim dynasties continued the tradition of book art.

Far East: This section highlights albums, scrolls, and decorative arts from China, Japan, and southeast Asia. From Japan, look for religious scrolls and eye-catching woodblock prints. From China, you might see a silk dragon robe of an emperor from the Qing dynasty (1644-1911), ornate snuff bottles, and rare jade books. The Qianlong emperor (r. 1736-1795)—a poet and arts patron—welcomed European Jesuits to his court and commissioned a huge collection of books, including some carved from jade. You also may see one of the few surviving volumes of a 16th-century copy of the Yongle Encyclopedia. Originally produced in the early 15th century, the encyclopedia was commissioned by the Yongle emperor to copy and collect all knowledge—from religion and philosophy to science and history—in one place.

Dublin's Cathedrals Area

Because of Dublin's English past (particularly Henry VIII's Reformation, and the dissolution of the Catholic monasteries in both Ireland and England in 1539), the city's top two churches are no longer Catholic. Christ Church Cathedral and nearby St. Patrick's Cathedral are both Church of Ireland (Anglican). In the late 19th century, the cathedrals underwent extensive restoration. The rich Guinness brewery family paid to try to make St. Patrick's Cathedral outshine Christ Church—whose patrons were a rival family of wealthy whiskey barons.

▲Christ Church Cathedral

Occupying the same site as the first wooden church built on this spot by the Christianized Viking chieftan Sitric Silkenbeard (c. 1030), the present structure is a mix of periods: Norman and Gothic, but mostly Victorian Neo-Gothic from the late 19th century.

Cost and Hours: €10, includes audioguide and crypt exhibition, €21 combo-ticket with Dublinia (described next); Mon-Sat 10:00-18:00, Sun 13:00-15:00 & 16:30-18:00, last entry 45 minutes before closing; occasional closures for special events; +353 1 677 8099, www.christchurchcathedral.ie.

Church Services and Evensong: There's a full Anglican service Sun at 11:00, and the public is welcome to a 45-minute evensong service, sung by the esteemed Christ Church choir (Thu at 18:00, Sun at 15:30).

Connecting Dublinia to the Cathedral: Note that if visiting both sights, the exit of Dublinia (on the top floor) puts you right onto an enclosed stone bridge that leads directly to the entry of Christ Church Cathedral (doesn't work in the other direction).

Visiting the Cathedral: The interior is Victorian, from the 1870s. Highlights are the finely carved wooden quire (with the grand bishop's seat) and the tomb of Strongbow, the Norman warlord who helped conquer Ireland, leading to centuries of British domination. (While he was buried here in 1176, this stone is a 14th-century replacement.) From the south transept, stairs lead down into the crypt—considered the oldest structure in town. Running the entire length of the church (with a forest of stout supporting columns), it's filled with historic odds and ends (and a WC).

▲Dublinia

This exhibit, which highlights Dublin's Viking and medieval past, is a hit with youngsters. It's cheesy but meaty enough for adults as well.

Cost and Hours: €15, €21 combo-ticket with Christ Church Cathedral; daily 10:00-17:30, last entry one hour before closing; ticket includes walking tour of medieval city surrounding the museum—daily at 11:00, 45 minutes; top-floor coffee shop, across from Christ Church Cathedral, +353 1 679 4611, www.dublinia.ie.

Visiting the Exhibits: The displays are laid out on three floors. The **ground floor** focuses on Viking Dublin, explaining life aboard a Viking ship and inside a Viking house. A Viking skeleton, excavated in 2003, slumbers in a glass case. Viking traders introduced urban life and commerce to Ireland—but kids may be more interested in their gory weaponry.

The **second floor** reveals day-to-day life in medieval Dublin, from merchant life to the town fair to nasty diseases, including leprosy and the plague. Like so much of Europe at that time (1347-1349), Ireland lost one-third of its population to the Black Death. The huge scale model of Dublin circa 1500 is well done.

The **top floor** features information about the area's archaeological excavations and a 3-D film fly-through of medieval Dublin. From this floor, you can climb a couple of flights of stairs into the tower for so-so views of Dublin, or exit across the bridge to Christ Church Cathedral.

▲St. Patrick's Cathedral

This Anglican cathedral is a thoughtful learning experience as well as a living church. The first church here was Catholic, supposedly built on the site where St. Patrick baptized local pagan converts. While the core of the Gothic structure you see today was built in the 13th century, most of today's stonework is 19th century. The building passed into the hands of the Anglican Church in the 16th century, after the Reformation. A century later, Oliver Cromwell's puritanical Calvinist troops—who considered the Anglicans to be little more than Catholics without a pope—stabled their horses here as a sign of disrespect.

Cost and Hours: €8, includes audioguide; Mon-Fri 9:30-17:00, Sat-Sun 9:00-18:00 except closed during Sun worship 10:30-13:00 & 14:30-16:30, shorter hours in off-season; free guided tours Mon-Fri at 10:30 and 14:30, possibly more—ask at front desk; at the intersection of Patrick Street and Upper Kevin Street, www.stpatrickscathedral.ie.

Evensong: You'll get chills listening to the local "choir of angels" (typically Mon-Fri at 17:30 and Sun at 15:15—but schedule can vary, especially in summer, when guest choirs perform; confirm on the church website, under Worship/Music Lists).

Visiting the Cathedral: The inside feels like an Irish version of Westminster Abbey, with venerable tombs and memorials to great Irish figures everywhere. The fine Victorian glass is from a Guinness-funded restoration in the 1870s. The regimental flags of the British army hang along the nave, colors slowly fading, in remembrance of soldiers lost. The north transept is home to a marble spiral staircase leading up to the loft of one of Ireland's largest organs. In the south transept is a delightful learning center about the life and history of the cathedral, along with thousand-year-old gravestones and free brass rubbing.

Jonathan Swift (author of *Gulliver's Travels*) was dean of the cathedral from 1713 to 1745. His grave and death mask are located near the front door (on the right side of the nave), where his cutting, self-penned epitaph reads: "Here lies the body of Jonathan Swift... Where savage indignation can no longer lacerate his heart."

▲▲Temple Bar

This much-promoted area—with shops, cafés, theaters, galleries, pubs with live music, and restaurants—feels like the heart of the old city. It's Dublin's touristy "Left Bank," on the south shore of the river, filling the cobbled streets between Dame Street and the River Liffey.

Three hundred years ago, this was the city waterfront, where tall sailing ships offloaded their goods (a "bar" was a loading dock along the river, and the Temples were a dominant merchant family). Eventually, the city grew eastward, filling in tidal mudflats, to create the docklands of modern Dublin. Once a thriving Georgian center of crafts-men and merchants, this neighborhood fell on hard times in the 20th century. Ensuing low rents attract-

ed students and artists, giving the area a bohemian flair.

With government tax incentives and lots of development money, the Temple Bar district has now become a thriving enter-tainment and beer-drinking hot spot. It can be an absolute spec-tacle in the evening, when it bursts with revelers. But even if you're just gawking, don't miss the opportunity to wander through this human circus.

Temple Bar Square, just off Temple Bar Street (near Ha' Penny Bridge), hosts street musicians and a Saturday book market. On busy weekends, people-watching here is a contact sport (and pick-pocketing is not). Farther west and somewhat hidden is Meeting House Square, with a lively food and produce market on Saturdays.

For more on sights in Temple Bar, see page 32; for pubs and music, see page 79.

Nearby: If the rowdy Temple Bar scene gets to be too much, cross over to the north bank of the River Liffey on the Millen-nium Bridge (next bridge west of the Ha' Penny Bridge), where you'll find a mellower, more cosmopolitan neighborhood with one-off shops and restaurants with outdoor seating in the **Millennium Walk district.**

NORTH OF THE RIVER LIFFEY

O'Connell Street, lined with statues of leading Irishmen, is the historic core north of the river. It's covered by the second half of my Dublin Walk, "O'Connell Street and Irish Heroes" (see page 34). And there's lots more to see. After you're oriented with the walk, consider the following sights.

▲▲EPIC: The Irish Emigration Museum

Telling the story of the Irish diaspora, this high-tech, interactive museum celebrates how this little island has had an oversized im-pact on the world. While the museum has few actual artifacts, this is an entertaining and educational experience. "EPIC" stands for "Every Person Is Connected."

Cost and Hours: €18.50, cheaper online, daily 10:00-18:45, last entry at 17:00, download audioguide for free or pay €2 to rent

DUBLIN

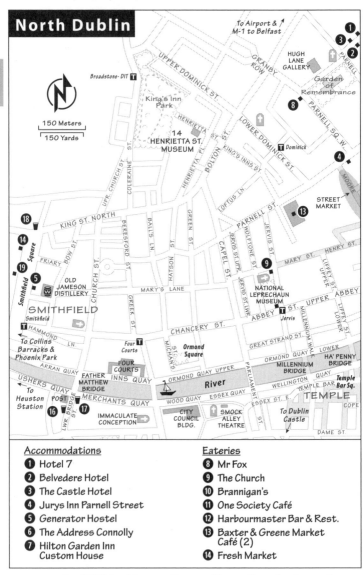

North Dublin

To Airport &
M-1 to Belfast

HUGH LANE GALLERY

Garden of Remembrance

Broadstone- DIT

King's Inn Park

150 Meters
150 Yards

14 HENRIETTA ST. MUSEUM

Dominick

STREET MARKET

KING ST. NORTH

Square

FRIARY

BOW ST.

OLD JAMESON DISTILLERY

MARY'S LANE

SMITHFIELD

Smithfield

HAMMOND LN.

To Collins Barracks & Phoenix Park

Four Courts

Ormond Square

FOUR COURTS

FATHER MATTHEW BRIDGE

INNS QUAY

CHANCERY ST.

MICHAN'S

GREAT STRAND ST.

ORMOND QUAY UPPER

ORMOND QUAY LOWER

MILLENNIUM BRIDGE

HA' PENNY BRIDGE

River

WOOD QUAY

ESSEX QUAY

WELLINGTON QUAY

Temple Bar Sq.

TEMPLE

ARRAN QUAY

USHERS QUAY

To Heuston Station

MERCHANTS QUAY

POST OFFICE

LWR. BRIDGE ST.

IMMACULATE CONCEPTION

CITY COUNCIL BLDG.

SMOCK ALLEY THEATRE

To Dublin Castle

DAME ST.

NATIONAL LEPRECHAUN MUSEUM

ABBEY ST.

Jervis

UPPER ABBEY

MARY ST.

HENRY ST.

CAPEL ST.

WOLFE TONE ST.

JERVIS ST. UPR.

JERVIS ST. LWR.

PARNELL ST.

JERVIS

MILLENNIUM WK.

PARNELL ST.

MOORE ST.

PARNELL SQ. W.

GRANBY ROW

UPPER DOMINICK ST.

LOWER DOMINICK ST.

HENRIETTA ST.

BOLTON ST.

KING'S INNS ST.

GREEN ST.

LOFTUS LN.

BERESFORD ST.

CHURCH ST.

GREEK ST.

MARY'S ABBEY

HALSTON ST.

COLERAINE ST.

UPR. CHURCH ST.

BALL'S LN.

Accommodations	Eateries
❶ Hotel 7	❽ Mr Fox
❷ Belvedere Hotel	❾ The Church
❸ The Castle Hotel	❿ Brannigan's
❹ Jurys Inn Parnell Street	⓫ One Society Café
❺ Generator Hostel	⓬ Harbourmaster Bar & Rest.
❻ The Address Connolly	⓭ Baxter & Greene Market Café (2)
❼ Hilton Garden Inn Custom House	⓮ Fresh Market

on-site, in the CHQ building on Custom House Quay (at the modern pedestrian bridge a few steps from the famine statues along the riverfront), +353 1 906 0861, www.epicchq.com.

Visiting the Museum: The museum fills the wine vaults in the basement of an iron-framed warehouse from the 1820s. Its 20 themed galleries feature videos, touchscreens, interactive tables, quizzes, etc. to explain the forces that propelled so many Irish around the globe. Featured illustrious emigrants include labor

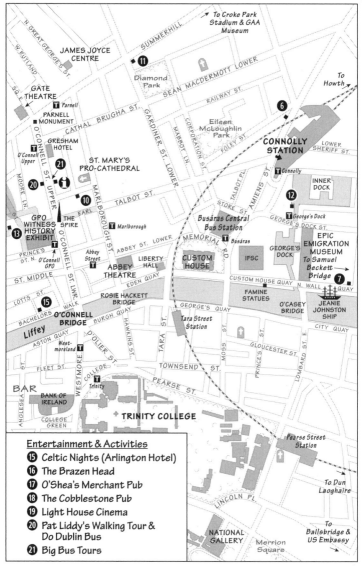

agitator Mother Jones, Caribbean pirate Anne Bonny, Australian bush bandit Ned Kelly, and musical Chicago police chief Francis O'Neill. Historic photos of filthy tenements and early films of bustling urban scenes document the plight of the common Irish emigrant. And all along you celebrate Irish heritage in music, literature, sports, and more.

Genealogy Help: The Irish Family History Centre on the ground floor can help you research your Irish roots via in-person or online consultations (€55/30 minutes, €95/hour, €135/1.5 hours, book ahead online, daily 10:30-17:30, +353 1 905 9216, www.irishfamilyhistorycentre.com).

Nearby: Looking downstream, notice the modern **Samuel Beckett Bridge**—shaped like an old Irish harp and designed by Santiago Calatrava. The areas north and south of this bridge have been rejuvenated over the last 30 years with strikingly modern buildings: on the north bank, with Dublin's contemporary convention center, and just inland from the south bank, with developments such as Google's European headquarters.

Before leaving the area, wander 50 yards up the River Liffey toward the city to contemplate the skeletal sculptures of the city's evocative **Famine Memorial.** Nearby you'll spot the masts of the *Jeanie Johnston* Tall Ship (see next). A visit here ties in well with the area's emigration theme.

▲*Jeanie Johnston* Tall Ship

Docked on the River Liffey, this seagoing sailing ship is a replica of a legendary Irish "famine ship." The original *Jeanie Johnston* embarked on 16 eight-week transatlantic crossings, carrying more than 2,500 Irish emigrants (about 200 per voyage) to their new lives in America and Canada in the decade after the Great Potato Famine of the 1840s. While many barely seaworthy hulks were known as "coffin ships," the people who boarded the *Jeanie Johnston* were lucky: The ship was Irish owned and crewed, with a humanitarian captain and even a doctor on board, and not one life was lost. Your tour guide will introduce you to the ship's main characters and help illuminate day-to-day life aboard a cramped tall ship 160 years ago.

Cost and Hours: €13, visits by 50-minute tour only, book in advance online; tours depart every 30 minutes Mon-Fri 10:00-16:30, every hour Sat-Sun 10:00-16:00, no tours at 13:00, shorter hours and fewer tours in winter; on the north bank of the Liffey just east of Sean O'Casey Bridge, +353 1 473 0111, www.jeaniejohnston.ie.

James Joyce Centre

Only aficionados of James Joyce's work will want to visit this micro-museum.

Cost and Hours: €5, Mon-Sat 10:00-17:00, Sun from 12:00, closed Mon in winter, 35 North Great George's Street, +353 1 878 8547, www.jamesjoyce.ie. Ask about walking tours of Joyce sights around Dublin.

Background: Born and raised in Dublin, James Joyce (1882-1941) wrote in great detail about his hometown and mined the local dialect for his pitch-perfect dialogue. His best-known work, *Ulysses,* chronicles one day in the life of the fictional Leopold Bloom as he wanders through the underside of Dublin. Joyce himself left Dublin (on June 17, 1904) for Paris and lived away from the city for most of his life. He never took up the cause of Irish nationalism and rarely delved into Irish mythology. He instead wrote with a new modernist focus on linguistic invention and social frankness.

Visiting the Center: Your visit spans three floors of a Georgian house. Among the exhibits, a re-creation of the messy, cramped study where Joyce wrote *Ulysses* evokes his struggles with poverty and criticism as he forged his own path. You'll see furniture from the Paris apartment of his friend Paul Léon, where Joyce spent much of his time while working on *Finnegan's Wake.* The center also features videos on Joyce's life and his enormous influence on subsequent writers, and an interactive exhibit tracing Bloom's Dublin odyssey.

Along the staircases, see portraits of Joyce and his wife and muse, Nora Barnacle. The first time they, um, went on a date was June 16, 1904. Joyce later set the events depicted in *Ulysses* on that date, which is commemorated annually as Bloomsday in Dublin. In a tiny back courtyard, you can see the original door from 7 Eccles Street, the address of Leopold Bloom.

Hugh Lane Gallery

This well-described exhibit of art from the 1870s onward includes a sampling of Impressionist masterpieces from the gallery's founding collection, once owned by Sir Hugh Lane, an Irish art dealer. Genteel and bite-size, the museum holds a well-known Monet painting (*Waterloo Bridge,* 1900), the reconstructed studio of Dublin-born modern artist Francis Bacon, and a few select works by Irish artists.

Cost and Hours: Free, Tue-Thu 10:00-18:00, Fri-Sat until 17:00, Sun 11:00-17:00, closed Mon, in the Dublin City Gallery on Parnell Square North, +353 1 222 5550, www.hughlane.ie.

▲GPO Witness History Exhibit

During the 1916 Easter Rising, Irish nationalists took over buildings in Dublin, including the General Post Office (GPO), which became the rebel headquarters. Initial euphoria led to chaotic street battles and ended with the grim realization among the insurgents that surrender was the best option—trusting that their martyrdom would inspire the country to rise more effectively. This engaging exhibit—in the working post office—is primarily focused on that pivotal Easter week. Additional exhibitions cover the related Irish War of Independence and the Irish Civil War.

Cost and Hours: €15, includes audioguide, Tue-Sat 10:00-17:00, closed Sun-Mon, last entry one hour before closing, +353 1 872 1916, www.gpowitnesshistory.ie.

Background: For European nations preoccupied with World War I, the Easter Rising was a sideshow—but it was critical to

Irish nationalists. Almost every Irish generation for the preceding 125 years had launched doomed insurrections against the British. But this one had a lasting effect, although it may not have seemed so in its immediate wake—a couple of weeks later, the patriot leaders who held their ground at the post office were executed in Kilmainham Gaol. Public sympathies shifted seismically. After seven centuries of dominance, the British were on a slippery slope leading to eventual independence for their nearest and oldest colony.

Visiting the Exhibit: The hardworking exhibit has a few interesting artifacts and lots of videos, photos, and earnest ways to tell the story. It features a fairly balanced view of the rebellion, including the less popular realities (like the lack of widespread support at the beginning of the movement and the civilians who died in the crossfire).

In the theater, watch the 17-minute widescreen video, "Fire and Steel"—a reenactment of the events that took place at different sites around the city that week. Find one of the interactive map stations, where you can zoom in and out of various Dublin neighborhoods for a day-by-day account of what was going on around the city. In video presentations, historians give their take on how the rebellion came about, and how it affected Irish history.

▲▲14 Henrietta Street

This four-story, 18th-century Georgian house, once an affluent mansion, had morphed into a cramped, impoverished, multifamily hovel by the 20th century. Now a museum—with visits by guided tour—it displays period architecture and furnishings, and explains tenement life and urban poverty in Dublin. With the help of photos and videos, your tour guide tells the story of the house and its times.

Cost and Hours: €10, visit by 75-minute guided tour only, book online in advance or take your chances; tours generally depart hourly Wed-Sun 10:00-16:00 (last tour time), closed Mon-Tue; 14 Henrietta Street, +353 1 524 0383, www.14henriettastreet.ie. They also offer a Georgian walking tour around the neighborhood (see website for times and to book ahead).

Visiting the House: Tours start on the top floor, where you'll learn about the aristocratic Molesworth family, who were the first occupants in the 1740s. In those days, Henrietta Street was the most exclusive enclave in Dublin, bringing balanced architectural order to this first Georgian-style lane on the rapidly expanding north side of the Liffey. Living luxuriously here, under ornate ceilings and warmed by fancy fireplaces, these privileged elite were unknowingly surrounding themselves with unhealthy choices: lead in the paint, arsenic in the wallpaper, and mercury in their makeup. Working your way down through the building, you learn how

From Famine to Revolution

After the Great Potato Famine (1845-1849), destitute rural Irish moved to the city in droves, seeking work and causing a housing shortage. Unscrupulous landlords came up with a solution: Subdivide the city's once-grand mansions, vacated by gentry after the 1801 Act of Union transferred all power to London. The mansions' tiny rooms could then be crammed with poor renters. Dublin became one of the most densely populated cities in Europe—one of every three Dubliners lived in a slum. On Henrietta Street, once a wealthy Dublin address, these new tenements bulged with humanity. According to the 1911 census, one district counted 835 people living in 15 houses (many with a single outhouse in back or even sharing a communal chamber pot). In these cramped, neglected quarters, tuberculosis was rampant, and infant mortality skyrocketed.

Those who could get work tenaciously clung to their precious jobs. The terrible working conditions prompted many to join trade unions, but when laborers went on strike in 1913, employers locked them out (the Dublin Lockout lasted for seven months). The picket lines were brutally put down by police in the pocket of rich businessmen, led by newspaper and hotel magnate William Murphy. In response, James Larkin and James Connolly formed the Irish Citizen Army, a militia, to protect the trade unionists.

Murphy eventually broke the unions. Larkin headed for the US to organize workers there. Meanwhile, Connolly stayed in Ireland and brought the Irish Citizen Army into the 1916 Easter Rising as an integral part of the rebel forces. During that uprising, he slyly had a rebel flag flown over Murphy's prized hotel on O'Connell Street. The uninformed British artillery battalions took the bait—and pulverized it.

the 1801 Act of Union pulled the plug on the good life: The Irish Parliament was dissolved, England asserted its rule, and the rich and politically well-connected moved to London. The house's once elegant rooms were subdivided, with entire families (many from the famine-wracked countryside) living in one room.

By 1911, there were more than 100 people living in this one house, split between 17 families sharing two toilets. On the basement level is a re-creation of the meager furnishings of an early 1900s flat. It's little wonder that Dublin's squalid tenements were the breeding ground for the socialist Irish Citizen Army militia of James Connolly, who fought fiercely in the 1916 Easter Rising. Rosie Hackett lived here at #14; the most famous woman in Connolly's army, she was a cofounder of the Irish Women Workers Union. Her name today adorns one of the bridges across the Liffey.

National Leprechaun Museum

This corny, low-tech attraction is fine for kids and lighthearted adults. On this 45-minute guided meander through Irish mythology, you'll visit a wishing well, a giant's living room, and a fairy fort, listening to tales that will enchant your wee ones.

Cost and Hours: €16, tours depart every 30 minutes Thu-Mon 10:30-17:30 (last tour time; also a few evenings—see below), closed Tue-Wed, a block north of the River Liffey on Abbey Street across from Jervis LUAS stop, +353 1 873 3899, www.leprechaunmuseum.ie.

Evening Visits: For adults only, a one-hour, interactive "Dark Land" storytelling performance explores the macabre side of Irish folklore (€18, Thu-Sat at 19:00 and 20:00 in summer).

Old Jameson Distillery

Whiskey fans enjoy visiting the old distillery. Your ticket includes a 40-minute tour covering the history of the distillery, the process of making whiskey, a tasting, and a drink. Unfortunately, the "distillery" feels corporate, overpriced, and put together for tourists. The Bushmills tour in Northern Ireland and the Midleton tour near Cork are better experiences.

Cost and Hours: €25 for guided tour, tours generally run every 15-30 minutes Mon-Thu 11:00-18:00, Fri-Sat until 19:00, Sun 12:00-18:00; specialty tours available—check their website for offerings, Bow Street, +353 1 807 2355, www.jamesonwhiskey.com.

Nearby: The neighborhood called **Smithfield** was on the fast track to gentrification prior to the 2008-2009 economic crash. Today, it's getting back on its feet and is home not only to the Old Jameson Distillery but also the best hostel lodging in town, the Light House art-film cinema, and The Cobblestone—Dublin's most authentic traditional-music pub (see page 80). All are on the long Smithfield Square, three blocks northwest of the Four Courts (Supreme Court building). The **Fresh Market,** near the top of the square, is a handy grocery stop for urban picnic fixings.

OUTER DUBLIN

Kilmainham Gaol and the Guinness Storehouse are located west of the old center and can be linked by a 20-minute walk, a five-minute taxi ride, or public bus #40 or #13. (To ride the bus from the jail to the Guinness Storehouse, leave the prison and take three rights—crossing no streets—to reach the bus stop.) Hop-on, hop-off buses also stop near both sights (see "Tours in Dublin" near the beginning of this chapter). For sight locations, see the "Dublin" map on page 8.

▲▲▲Kilmainham Gaol

Opened in 1796 as Dublin's county jail and a debtors' prison, Kilmainham was considered a model in its day. In reality, the British frequently used this jail as a political prison. Many of those who fought for Irish independence were held or executed here, including leaders of the rebellions of 1798, 1803, 1848, 1867, and 1916. James Connolly, unable to stand in front of the firing squad because of a gangrenous ankle, was tied to a chair and shot sitting down. National heroes Robert Emmett and Charles Stewart Parnell each did time here. The last prisoner to be held in the jail was Éamon de Valera, who later became president of Ireland. He was released  on July 16, 1924, the day Kilmainham was finally shut down. The buildings, virtually in ruins, were restored in the 1960s and opened as a museum in 1966.

Cost and Hours: €8, visit by one-hour guided tour only, advance booking highly recommended; daily 9:30-17:45, June-Aug until 18:15, Oct-March until 17:15; +353 1 453 5984, www.kilmainhamgaolmuseum.ie.

Advance Tickets Recommended: Book online at least a few days in advance to guarantee a spot on a tour. If you want to buy a same-day ticket, check their website around 9:15-9:30, which is when they release canceled tickets. You can try just showing up, but you may get turned away.

Getting There: Hop-on, hop-off buses stop near here, or take bus #69 or #79 from Aston Quay or #13 or #40 from O'Connell Street or College Green—confirm with driver. The closest LUAS tram stop is Suir Road (red line, zone 1 ticket from city center). From there, it's a 10-minute, level walk north, crossing over the Grand Canal, to the jail.

Visiting the Jail: Your visit starts in the prison's Catholic chapel with some background and history. From there, your guide leads you through the dark and claustrophobic West Wing (the oldest part of the jail), into the open and light-filled Victorian East Wing, and through the Stonebreakers' Yard, where hard labor was performed and executions took place. It's sobering to tour the cells and places of execution—hearing tales of oppressive colonialism and heroic patriotism—alongside Irish schoolkids who know these names well.

After the tour, you can explore the museum, which has an excellent exhibit on Victorian prison life and Ireland's fight for independence. Don't miss the dimly lit "Last Words 1916" hall upstairs, which displays the stirring final letters that patriots sent to loved ones hours before facing the firing squad. Regrettably, transcriptions of the letters are not posted, denying visitors a better understanding of the passion and patriotism of Ireland's greatest in their own last words—a lost opportunity for Americans not realizing that there are other Nathan Hales in this world who wish they had more than one life to give for their country. (You may be able to find the inspirational *Last Words* book in the bookshop.)

Nearby: Across the street from the jail is the **Irish Museum of Modern Art** (IMMA), set in a pretty green park and free to visit (www.imma.ie).

▲Guinness Storehouse

A visit to the Guinness Storehouse is, for many, a pilgrimage. Arthur Guinness began brewing the renowned stout here in 1759, and by 1868 it was the biggest brewery in the world. Today, the sprawling complex fills several city blocks (64 acres busy brewing 1.5 million pints a day).

Visitors (1.5 million annually) are welcomed to the towering storehouse, where the vibe is glitzy entertainment. Don't look for conveyor belts of beer bottles being stamped with bottle caps. Rather than a brewery tour, this is a Disneyland for beer lovers—huge crowds, high decibel music, and dreamy TV beer ads on big screens.

Cost and Hours: €26-30 for access to building and a drink in the Gravity Bar (higher prices Thu-Sun); even pricier tickets add extra tastings and experiences—see website for options; Mon-Thu 10:00-19:00, Fri-Sat 9:30-20:00, Sun 9:30-19:00, shorter hours off-season, last entry two hours before closing, last beer served 45 minutes before closing; bring earbuds to listen to audio info on your phone; entrance is mid-block on Market Street South, +353 1 408 4800, www.guinness-storehouse.com.

Advance Tickets Recommended: The brewery is popular with cruise-ship excursions, making an advance ticket the only smart way to visit. Book your timed-entry slot early or late in the day to avoid the mobs.

Getting There: Ride the hop-on, hop-off bus (it stops near the site), or take bus #13, #40, or #123 from Dame Street and O'Connell Street. The St. James' Hospital LUAS stop on the red line is a 15-minute walk west of the Storehouse.

Eating: There are several eateries at the brewery, including an

The Famous Record-Breaking Records Book

Look up "beer" in the *Guinness World Records,* and you'll discover that the record for removing beer bottle caps with one's teeth is 68 in one minute. But aside from listing records for amazing—or amazingly stupid—feats, this famous record book has a more subtle connection with beer.

In 1951, while hunting in Ireland's County Wexford, Sir Hugh Beaver, then the managing director at Guinness Breweries, got into a debate with his companions over which was the fastest game bird in Europe: the golden plover or the red grouse. That night at his estate, after scouring many reference books, they were disappointed not to find a definitive answer.

Beaver realized that similar questions were likely being debated nightly in pubs across Ireland and Britain. So he hired a fact-finding team in London to compile a book of answers to various questions. In 1955, the *Guinness Book of Records* (later renamed *Guinness World Records*) was published. By Christmas, it topped the British bestseller list.

In the beginning, entries mostly focused on natural phenomena and animal oddities, but grew to include a wide variety of extreme human achievements.

The iconic book is now available in more than 100 countries and 40 languages, with more than 150 million copies sold to date. As the bestselling copyrighted book of all time, it even earns a record-breaking entry within its own pages.

easy to-go café on the second floor; on the fifth floor, you'll find modern Irish food at the 1837 Bar & Brasserie, and simpler fare at Arthur's Bar.

Visiting the Brewery: Enter the brewery on Market Street South. The exhibit fills the old fermentation plant, used from 1902 through 1988, and reopened in 2000 as a huge shrine to the Guinness tradition. Step into the middle of the ground floor and look up. A tall, beer-glass-shaped glass atrium—14 million pints big (that's about 10 days' worth of production) soars seven stories upward past floors of exhibitions to the skylight. Then look down at Arthur's original 9,000-year lease, enshrined under Plexiglas in the floor. At £45 per year, it was quite a bargain.

As you escalate ever higher, you'll notice that each floor has a theme. Scan the QR codes posted throughout to bring up audio information for the exhibits. The first couple of floors explain the making of Guinness, from the ingredients to the brewing process. One exhibit is dedicated to cooperage, the making of wooden barrels (with 1954 film clips showing master kegmakers working at their now virtually extinct trade).

The second floor has the tasting rooms (you may have to wait in line to get in). In the White Room you're introduced to using your five senses to appreciate the perfect porter. Then, in the Velvet Chamber, you're taught how to taste it from a leprechaun-sized beer glass.

The third floor features fun advertising Guinness has created over the years. The fourth floor is for special experiences (at an extra cost), such as learning how to pull your own beer or getting your image printed on a head of beer. The fifth floor has a couple of eateries. The top-floor Gravity Bar provides visitors with a commanding 360-degree view of Dublin—with vistas all the way to the sea—and an included pint of the beloved stout.

Claiming Your Beer: Your admission includes a ticket for a beer, which you can claim either at Arthur's Bar (fifth floor, more drink options) or the Gravity Bar (top floor, most energy and fun plus great views). Among your choices are basic stout (4.2%), Hop House 13 (5%, a hoppy lager), and Nitro IPA (5.8%, bitter and hoppy). At Arthur's, you have more options, such as extra stout (4.1%, carbonated), Dublin Porter (3.8%, 1796 recipe), West Indies Porter (6%, toffee flavor, 1801 recipe), or Black Velvet (Prosecco and Guinness).

Whiskey Distilleries in The Liberties

Irish whiskey is undergoing a revival, and in recent years, several craft distilleries have opened their doors for tours, tastings, and special experiences. The heart of the new whiskey wave is in The Liberties, the brewing and distilling center of Dublin during the 19th century. While Guinness survived, the distilleries all closed in the 20th century and only now are coming back to life. The first two are located just a couple of minutes from the Guinness Storehouse; Teeling is closer to the center of town. Check distillery websites for tour times, specifics, and to book ahead.

Roe & Co Whiskey Distillery, from the company that owns Guinness, is named for and located on the site of one of the 19th-century pioneers of Irish whiskey, George Roe & Co. They offer two 40-minute tours—one focused on cocktails, the other on blending—followed by time in their bar (tours run Thu-Sun, 92 James's Street, www.roeandcowhiskey.com).

Just down the street is **Pearse Lyons,** named after its founder, an Irishman who made his fortune in Kentucky bourbons, among other things. Pearse Lyons is located in a renovated 12th-century church; tours go through the graveyard and into the church, where the bar and distillery equipment are housed (tours run Wed-Mon, 121 James's Street, +353 1 691 6000, www.pearselyonsdistillery.com).

About a 10-minute walk from Guinness toward the city

center is **Teeling Distillery,** whose opening in 2015 helped kick off Dublin's whiskey revival. Various tours offer different levels of tastings (tours daily, 13 Newmarket, +353 1 531 0888, www. teelingdistillery.com).

▲National Museum of Decorative Arts and History

This branch of the National Museum, which occupies the huge, 18th-century stone Collins Barracks in west Dublin, displays Irish dress, furniture, weapons, silver, and other domestic baubles from the past 700 years. History buffs will linger longest in the Soldiers & Chiefs exhibit, which covers the Irish at war both at home and abroad since 1500 (including the American Civil War). The sober finale is the Proclaiming a Republic room, offering Ireland's best coverage of the painful birth of this nation. Guns, flags, and personal letters help illustrate the 1916 Easter Rising, the War of Independence against Britain, and Ireland's Civil War. Also on the museum grounds is the historic *Asgard*, a 51-foot yacht used by its owner, Erskine Childers, to smuggle guns to arm Irish rebels in the 1916 Easter Rising. You'll find the boat 50 yards across a small parking lot in a well-marked separate building.

Cost and Hours: Free, Tue-Sat 10:00-17:00, Sun-Mon from 13:00, good café; on north side of the River Liffey in Collins Barracks on Benburb Street, roughly across the river from Guinness Storehouse, LUAS red line: Museum stop; +353 1 677 7444, www. museum.ie.

▲Gaelic Athletic Association Museum at Croke Park Stadium

This museum, at Croke Park Stadium in northeast Dublin, offers a high-tech, interactive introduction to Ireland's favorite games. The GAA, founded in 1884, was created to foster the development of Gaelic sports, specifically Gaelic football and hurling, and to exclude English sports such as cricket and rugby (see sidebar). An expression of the Irish cultural awakening, the GAA played an important part in the fight for independence. Relive the greatest moments in hurling and Irish-football history. Then get involved: Pick up a stick and try hurling, kick a football, and test your speed and balance. A 15-minute film (played on request) gives you a "Sunday at the stadium" experience. It's also fun to take in an actual hurling or football match (see below).

Cost and Hours: €8, Mon-Sat 9:30-17:00, Sun from 10:00, may be closed on some Sat-Sun if there's a match—check ahead, +353 1 819 2300, www.crokepark.ie/gaa-museum.

Getting There: Croke Park is located on the north bank of the Royal Canal, about 10 blocks north of the Connolly train station. The museum is located under the stands at the stadium (enter from

St. Joseph's Avenue off Clonliffe Road). From the city center, it's about a 30-minute walk. Or you can take bus #40 or a taxi.

Tours: The €15 Stadium Tour is worth it for rabid fans who want a glimpse of the huge stadium and locker rooms (80 minutes). The €21 rooftop Skyline Tour offers views 17 stories above the field from lofty catwalks (1.5 hours). Both tours include museum entry and run several times daily (fewer tours on match days); see the website for times and to book.

Watching Hurling or Football: Actually seeing a match at Croke Park, surrounded by incredibly spirited Irish fans, is a fun experience. Hurling is fast and rough: like airborne hockey with no injury time-outs. Gaelic football resembles a rugged form of soccer; you can carry the ball, but must bounce or kick it every three steps. Matches are held most Saturday or Sunday afternoons in summer (May-Aug), culminating in the hugely popular all-Ireland finals on Sunday afternoons in August. Choose a county to support, buy their colors to wear or wave, scream yourself hoarse, and you'll be a temporary local (tickets around €20-55, buy in advance at www.gaa.ie, no on-site ticket sales).

Glasnevin Cemetery

This is the final resting place for Ireland's most passionate patriots, writers, politicians, and assorted personalities. What Père Lachaise is to Paris, Glasnevin is to Dublin. Here you'll find the graves of Michael Collins, Charles Stewart Parnell, teenage rebel and martyr Kevin Barry (of patriot song fame), and Daniel O'Connell, whose crypt lies beneath a commemorative tower (recently renovated and climbable). A tall wall and a half-dozen watchtowers, used to deter grave robbers, surround the cemetery's 124 leafy acres.

The adjacent visitors center offers more exploration, including an exhibition on the famous figures buried at Glasnevin and an overview of the cemetery's history. The visitors center also runs guided cemetery tours.

Cost and Hours: Cemetery—free, open daily 8:00-18:00; visitors center exhibition—€6, daily 10:00-17:00; tour-€13, tour/tower climb-€18, tours depart daily at 11:30 and 14:30 and include exhibit entry; café, +353 1 882 6550, www.dctrust.ie/experience-glasnevin.html.

Getting There: It's two miles north of the city center, along Finglas Road—take bus #40 or #140 from the GPO on O'Connell Street.

Gaelic Athletic Association

The Gaelic Athletic Association (GAA) has long been a powerhouse in Ireland. The national pastimes of Gaelic football

and hurling pack stadiums all over the country. When you consider that 82,000 people—paying about €25 each—stuff Dublin's Croke Park Stadium and that all the athletes are strictly amateur, you might wonder, "Where does all the money go?"

Ireland has a long tradition of using the revenue generated by these huge events to promote Gaelic athletics and Gaelic culture in a grassroots and neighborhood way. So, while the players (many of whom are schoolteachers whose jobs allow for evenings and summers free) participate only for the glory of their various counties, the money generated is funding children's leagues, school coaches, small-town athletic facilities, and traditional arts, music, and dance—as well as the building and maintenance of giant stadiums such as Croke Park.

Sports here have a deep emotional connection as a heartfelt expression of Irish identity. There was a time when membership in the GAA was denied to anyone who also attended "foreign games," defined as rugby, soccer, or cricket. If the Brits played it, it was viewed as cultural poison. So intractable was this rule that in 1938, Douglas Hyde (then president of Ireland) was kicked out of the GAA for attending an international soccer match. (The rule was abolished in 1971 with the advent of TV sports.)

In 1921, during the War of Independence, IRA leader Michael Collins orchestrated the simultaneous assassination of a dozen British intelligence agents around Dublin in a single morning. The same day, the Black and Tans retaliated. These grizzled British WWI veterans, clad in black police coats and tan surplus army pants, had been sent to Ireland to stamp out the rebels. Knowing Croke Park would be full of Irish nationalists, they entered the packed stadium during a Gaelic football match and fired into the stands, killing 13 spectators as well as a Tipperary player.

Today Croke Park's "Hill 16" grandstands are built on rubble dumped here after the 1916 Easter Rising; it's literally sacred ground. And the Hogan stands are named after the murdered player from Tipperary. Queen Elizabeth II visited the stadium during her historic visit in 2011. Her warm interest in the stadium and in the institution of the GAA did much to heal old wounds.

Dublin for Kids

If the youngsters in your clan need a break from Dublin's literary sights, ancient Celtic artifacts, medieval churches, and urban rebel hideouts, try sprinkling in some of these activities.

Dublinia Kid-friendly coverage of grisly Viking history (see page 59).

Viking Splash Tours Rowdy ride through Dublin history in a WWII amphibious vehicle—driven by a Viking-costumed guide who spouts jokes and historic factoids as you ramble across town (€25 for adults, €20 for students, €15 for ages 3-14, daily 10:00-18:00 in summer, https://vikingsplashdublin.ie).

National Leprechaun Museum Irish mythology for impressionable wee ones (see page 68).

Jeanie Johnston **Tall Ship** The experience of an Atlantic voyage of emigration told by role-playing swabbies aboard a replica sailing ship (see page 64).

Irish Rock 'n' Roll Museum The evolution of Irish rock music and studio memorabilia (see page 33).

Gaelic Athletic Association Museum High-tech Gaelic football and hurling exhibits at Croke Park Stadium—including a chance to whack the ball in the hurling equivalent of a batting cage (see page 73).

Phoenix Park Rent bikes in this gigantic safe-to-cycle greenbelt (includes a zoo; see page 7).

Gravedigger Ghost Tour This ghoulish bus tour is catnip for teens but too spooky for little ones (www.thegravedigger.ie).

St. Stephen's Green Kid-friendly park (feed the ducks) and secret stress reducer for mom and dad (see page 18).

Eddie Rocket's Diner This burger-and-shake franchise (there are several in central Dublin) is a step above fast food for finicky kids needing a slurp of home (www.eddierockets.ie).

Shopping in Dublin

Smaller shops are open roughly Monday-Saturday 10:00-18:00 with shorter hours or possibly closures on Sunday. Department stores generally have longer hours.

Department Stores: The dominant department store in Dublin (and Ireland) is **Dunnes,** where you can buy everything from groceries to underwear to alcohol. Some Dunnes branches are grocery stores only; department stores are at the Stephen's Green Shopping Center (near St. Stephen's Green) and in North Dublin, a couple of blocks west of O'Connell Street (48 Henry Street, www.dunnesstores.com).

Irish Crafts and Design: Dublin has a number of good shops for browsing locally made goods. The **Kilkenny Shop,** across from Trinity College, focuses on Irish designers, including clothing, jewelry, and home goods (6 Nassau Street, good cafeteria upstairs, www.kilkennyshop.com).

Avoca is a mini department store loaded with quality Irish crafts and food. They weave their own woolens at their mill in Wicklow, and they are a fine place to look for scarves and blankets (11 Suffolk Street, www.avoca.com).

Powerscourt Center occupies a Georgian house and elegant courtyard near Grafton Street. Shops are a mix of local retailers and international chains selling jewelry, clothing, housewares, paper goods, and local Irish arts and crafts (59 William Street South, www.powerscourtcentre.ie).

The **Irish Design Shop** offers an array of Ireland-made products, including cookbooks, art, ceramics, soaps, blankets, scarves, and jewelry (41 Drury Street, www.irishdesignshop.com). Nearby are a couple of design shops selling mostly international brands but also some locally made items: **Industry & Co** (41a/b Drury Street, www.industryandco.com) and **Designist** (68 South Great George's Street, www.designist.ie).

Jewelry: Pendants, earrings, and other pieces featuring shamrocks, Celtic knots, and the Tree of Life are ubiquitous in Dublin. Also popular is the traditional Claddagh ring that symbolizes love, loyalty, and friendship (most popular in Galway, where the ring originated). There are plenty of stores in town selling Celtic jewelry, but a quality place for tasteful designs in a range of prices and materials is **Weir & Sons** (#96 Grafton Street, www.weirandsons. ie).

For more contemporary pieces, browse **The Collective,** which highlights 30 or so independent jewelry designers, many of whom are Irish (24 Drury Street, www.thecollectivedublin.ie).

Bookstores: With its rich literary history, Dublin is a fun place to shop for books. South of the Liffey, try **Dubray Books** on Grafton Street (at #36, www.dubraybooks.ie); **Hodges Figgis,** founded in 1768 and mentioned in *Ulysses* (56 Dawson Street, www.waterstones.com/bookshops/hodges-figgis); and the **Gutter Bookshop,** a fine independent seller that champions Irish writers (Cow's Lane in Temple Bar, www.gutterbookshop.com). In North Dublin you'll find **Eason's** (5 minutes north of the O'Connell Bridge at 40 O'Connell Street Lower, www.easons.com; they also have other branches around town).

Shopping Areas
If you're in the mood to browse, try the following streets and neighborhoods.

South Dublin: Pedestrianized **Grafton Street** is lined with international chain stores and a few local shops. Near Grafton are shopping centers (Powerscourt Center—described above—and Stephen's Green Shopping Center); arcades (Great George's Arcade between Great George's and Drury Streets); and shopping streets (Drury Street—good artisan and design shops—and Francis Street, creaking with antiques).

Nassau Street, lining Trinity College, is home to the popular Kilkenny Shop (described above) and lots of touristy stores.

Temple Bar, the big nightlife spot, is worth a browse for art, jewelry, books, and gift shops. On Saturdays, a couple of markets—one for food and another for books—set up shop. For details on this area, see pages 60 and 79.

North Dublin: Dublin's top department stores are on **Henry Street** (pedestrian-only, off O'Connell Street).

Millennium Walk, a trendy lane stretching two blocks north from the River Liffey to Abbey Street, is filled with hip restaurants, shops, and coffee bars. It's easy to miss—look for the south entry at the pedestrian Millennium Bridge, or the north entry at the Jervis Street LUAS stop.

Entertainment in Dublin

Ireland has produced some of the finest writers in the English and Irish languages, and Dublin houses some of Europe's best theaters. Though the city was the site of the first performance of Handel's *Messiah* (1742), these days Dublin is famous for the rock bands that have started here: U2, Thin Lizzy, Sinéad O'Connor, and Bob Geldof's band The Boomtown Rats.

Theater

Abbey Theatre is Ireland's national theater, founded by W. B. Yeats in 1904 to preserve Irish culture during British rule. Besides plays, they also do backstage and walking tours (26 Lower Abbey Street, +353 1 878 7222, www.abbeytheatre.ie). **Gate Theatre** does foreign plays as well as Irish classics (Cavendish Row, +353 1 874 4045, www.gatetheatre.ie). The **Gaiety Theatre** offers a wide range of quality productions (King Street South, +353 1 679 5622, www.gaietytheatre.ie). The **Bord Gáis Energy Theatre** (pronounced "Board-GOSH") is Dublin's newest and spiffiest venue (Grand Canal Square, +353 1 677 7999, www.bordgaisenergytheatre.ie). Less commercial plays can be seen at the intimate little **Smock Alley Theatre,** with seating surrounding a tiny stage, in a space on the site of the city's first theater—from 1662 (6 Lower Exchange Street, on the western fringe of Temple Bar, +353 1 677 0014, www.smockalley.com). Check online or at the TI to see what's on.

Music, Dance, and Film

The 3 Arena, sited on what was once a dock railway terminus (easy LUAS red line access), is now sponsored by a hip phone company. Residents call it by its geographic nickname: The Point. It's considered one of the country's top live-music venues (East Link Bridge, +353 1 819 8888, http://3arena.ie).

The **National Concert Hall** supports a varied performance schedule, including the National Symphony Orchestra on most Friday evenings (off St. Stephen's Green at Earlsfort Terrace, +353 1 417 0077, www.nch.ie).

Celtic Nights combines traditional music and dancing into a big-stage, high-energy, family-friendly, Irish variety show. This touristy dinner act hits all the clichés, from *Riverdance*-style choreography to fun fiddling and comedic *craic*. It comes with a traditional three-course dinner and lots of audience participation (€42.90, nightly show at 20:30, on the north side of the river by the O'Connell Bridge at the Arlington Hotel, 23 Bachelors Walk—see map on page 62, +353 1 687 5200, www.celticnights.com).

The **Irish Film Institute,** bordering Meeting House Square in Temple Bar, shows a variety of art-house flicks. A bohemian crowd relaxes in its bar/café, awaiting the next film (main entry at 6 Eustace Street, www.irishfilm.ie).

Pubs and Live Traditional Music

James Joyce once said it would be a good puzzle to try to walk across Dublin without passing a pub. For guided pub crawls (focusing on either Irish literature or music), see "Tours in Dublin," near the beginning of this chapter. Unless otherwise noted, for locations of the venues described below, see the "South Dublin Restaurants" map on page 90. The music start times listed below tend to be loose.

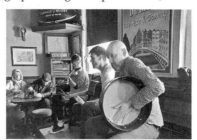

Temple Bar and Nearby

The Temple Bar area thrives with music—traditional, jazz, and rock. Pricier than the rest of Dublin and extremely touristy, it's a wild scene and—for party animals—a good place to mix beer and music. The noise, pushy crowds, and inflated prices have driven most local Dubliners away. It's craziest on summer weekend nights, holidays, and nights after big sporting events let out. Women in funky hats, part of loud "hen" (bachelorette) parties, promenade down the main drag as drunken dudes shout from pub doorways to get their attention.

In the most touristy zone around Temple Bar Square, the bars are cartoons of an Irish pub, looking like they board leprechauns upstairs. The only real Irish people you'll see are the ones playing the music, serving the beer, and keeping the rowdies at bay at the doorway. But several good pubs for traditional music are nearby—a 10-minute hike up the river west of Temple Bar takes you to a more local and less touristy scene. The pubs there have longer histories, tangled floor plans, a fun-loving energy, and a passion for trad.

Gogarty's Pub has long been the leading Temple Bar pub for trad. They have foot-tapping sessions downstairs (Wed-Sun from 13:00 until late) and upstairs (Sat-Sun from 17:00; at corner of Fleet and Anglesea, +353 1 671 1822). This is also where the **Traditional Irish Musical Pub Crawl** starts (see page 13).

Darkey Kelly's Bar is a big, fun-loving place with live music nightly. The traditional folk-music vibe here is more sing-along than hard drinking, and the pub grub is good. See their website for what's on when (daily from about 19:30, west end of Temple Bar, near Christ Church Cathedral at 19 Fishamble Street, +353 83 346 4682, https://darkeykellys.ie).

The Brazen Head, which claims to be the oldest pub in Dublin, is a hit for an early dinner and late live music (good food, music nightly from 21:30), with atmospheric rooms and a courtyard perfect for balmy evenings (by south end of Father Mathew Bridge, 2 blocks west of Christ Church Cathedral at 20 Lower Bridge Street—see map on page 62; +353 1 679 5186).

The Stag's Head, a Victorian-era pub, hosts "An Evening of Irish Folklore and Fairies," an hour and a half of soulful history and fascinating mythology. Soaking up a pint while enjoying engaging Irish storytelling is a fine way to kick off your evening (€23, food and drinks extra; generally Tue and Thu at 17:00, reservations required, 1 Dame Court—see map on page 84, +353 1 218 8555, www.irishfolktours.com).

O'Shea's Merchant Pub, across the street, is encrusted with memories of County Kerry football heroes. It's popular with locals who come for the live traditional music nightly (around 21:00 or 22:00; the front half is a restaurant, the toe-tapping magic is in the back—enter at 12 Lower Bridge Street—see map on page 62, +353 1 679 3797, www.themerchanttemplebar.com).

North of the River
The Cobblestone Pub offers Dublin's least glitzy and most rewarding traditional-music scene. It's in Smithfield, near Jameson, so it's a taxi ride for most people—but it's worth the trouble. Stepping

inside during a session is like entering another world—friendly and untouristy. The walls, covered with photos of honored trad musicians, set the tone. Music is revered here, as reflected in the understated sign: "Listening area, please respect musicians" (trad-music sessions weeknights from about 19:00, weekends from about 17:00; 100 yards from Old Jameson Distillery's brick chimney tower at 77 King Street North, +353 1 872 1799, www.cobblestonepub.ie). For location, see the "North Dublin" map on page 62.

Southeast of St. Stephen's Green
Down the axis of Merrion Row and Lower Baggot Street, you'll find three venerable pubs (within a block of each other) filled with businessmen and staff from nearby governmental buildings blowing off steam. One is great for music. All are great for beer lovers. For locations, see the "Southeast Dublin" map on page 86.

O'Donoghue's was famously the home pub of the Dubliners, for decades one of Ireland's premier traditional Irish-music groups. The pub still offers a happy scene and nightly music (trad, folk, more) from 20:00 (15 Merrion Row, +353 1 660 7194).

Doheny & Nesbitt is a photogenic choice, with wonderful woodwork and cozy conversational alcoves—and it has great pub grub (5 Lower Baggot Street, +353 1 676 2945).

Toner's is another well-varnished choice—it's already celebrated its 200th anniversary. It has the added attraction of a classic snug in front and a large beer garden out back, mostly to accommodate smokers (139 Lower Baggot Street, +353 1 676 3090).

Sister Pubs near Trinity College
See the map on page 90 for locations.

Porterhouse Central Bar has an inviting and varied menu (tacos, burgers, pizzas) and Dublin's best selection of microbrews. It's not as sloppy as Temple Bar but still loud and with a fun energy. This is a good place for a pub dinner. You won't find Guinness here, just tasty homebrews. Try one of their three-beer samplers (45 Nassau Street, +353 1 679 9204, check music schedule at www.theporterhouse.ie).

The Dingle Whiskey Bar boasts its namesake libation but also features 180 whiskeys from Ireland, Scotland, and North America. The ceiling is lined with staves inscribed with the names of investors who've bought a barrel and are waiting years for it to age. Tasting flights are available for novice to connoisseur palates (44 Nassau Street, +353 1 677 4180).

Sleeping in Dublin

Choosing the right neighborhood in Dublin is as important as choosing the right hotel. All of my recommended accommodations are in safe areas convenient to sightseeing.

Central Dublin is popular, loud, and expensive. You'll find big, practical, central places south of the river, near Christ Church Cathedral, Trinity College, and St. Stephen's Green. For classy, older accommodations in a quieter neighborhood, stay a bit farther out, southeast of St. Stephen's Green. North of the river are additional reliable options in an urban area well served by LUAS trams (but less personal and with less personality). If you're on a tight budget, get a room in outlying Dun Laoghaire or Howth (see the end of this chapter), where rooms are cheaper—and quieter (both an easy 25-minute DART train ride into the city).

I rank accommodations from $ budget to $$$$ splurge. For the best deal, contact small hotels directly by phone or email. When you book direct, the owner avoids a commission and may be able to offer a discount. Prices are often discounted on weeknights (Mon-Thu) and from November through February. For some travelers, short-term, Airbnb-type rentals can be a good alternative; search for places in my recommended hotel neighborhoods.

Book your Dublin accommodations well in advance, especially if you'll be traveling during peak season (June-August), weekends any time of year, or if your trip coincides with a major holiday or festival (see the appendix). Hotels raise their prices and are packed on rugby weekends (about four per year), during the all-Ireland Gaelic football and hurling finals (Sundays in August), and during summer rock concerts.

For more details on reservations, short-term rentals, and more, see the "Sleeping" section in the Practicalities chapter.

SOUTH OF THE RIVER LIFFEY
Near Christ Church Cathedral
$$$$ Jurys Inn Christ Church, part of a no-nonsense, American-style hotel chain, is central and offers business-class comfort in 182 identical rooms. If "ye olde" is getting old—and you don't mind big tour groups—this is a good option. Request a room far from the noisy elevator (breakfast extra, book long in advance for weekends, pay parking nearby, Christ Church Place, opposite Christ Church Cathedral, +353 1 454 0000, www.jurysinns.com, jurysinnchristchurch@jurysinns.com). If staying here, consider eating breakfast at one of the small cafés nearby; try the Queen of Tarts or Chorus Café (see listings under "Eating in Dublin," later).

Trinity College Area

You can't get more central than Trinity College; these listings offer a good value for the money.

$$$$ Trinity Townhouse offers fine, quiet lodging in 31 rooms split between Georgian townhouses on either side of South Frederick Street, just south of Trinity College (three floors, no elevator, 29 South Frederick Street, +353 1 617 0900, www. trinitytownhousehotel.ie, reception@trinitytownhouse.ie).

$$$ Trinity College opens its 700 student-housing dorm rooms to the public in summer (late May-mid-Aug). There are en-suite rooms as well as rooms within apartments with a shared kitchen, living room, and bathroom—good for families or groups (make sure to book rooms for the city center campus, not suburban Dartry location, breakfast extra, +353 1 896 1177, www.tcd.ie/summeraccommodation, reservations@tcd.ie).

Near St. Stephen's Green

$$$$ Brooks Hotel is a fine choice for great service, tending 98 plush rooms in an ideal central location. This splurge rarely disappoints (breakfast extra, elevator, Drury Street, +353 1 670 4000, www.brookshotel.ie, reservations@brookshotel.ie).

$$$$ Buswells Hotel, one of the city's oldest, is a pleasant Georgian-style haven with 67 rooms in the heart of the city (breakfast extra, between Trinity College and St. Stephen's Green at 23 Molesworth Street, +353 1 614 6500, www.buswells.ie, info@buswells.ie).

$$$ Albany House's 57 good-value rooms come with high ceilings, Georgian ambience, and some stairs. Ask for a quieter room in back, away from streetcar noise (one block south of St. Stephen's Green at 84 Harcourt Street, +353 1 475 1092, www.albanyhousedublin.com, info@albanyhousedublin.com).

$$$ Fitzwilliam Townhouse rents 17 renovated rooms in a Georgian townhouse near St. Stephen's Green (family rooms, breakfast extra, 41 Upper Fitzwilliam Street, +353 1 662 5155, www.fitzwilliamtownhouse.com, info@fitzwilliamtownhouse.com).

Southeast of St. Stephen's Green

The Grand Canal, Dublin's urban waterway, sports a lovely narrow greenbelt of trees and lily pads ideal for a pleasant stroll or run. This neighborhood—stretching roughly east-west from Leeson Street to Grand Canal Street—is a perfect compromise between busy central lodging options and more sedate choices farther out. Some of these listings are unique places, and they charge accordingly. If you're going to break the bank, do it here.

$$$$ Number 31 is a hidden gem reached via gritty little

DUBLIN

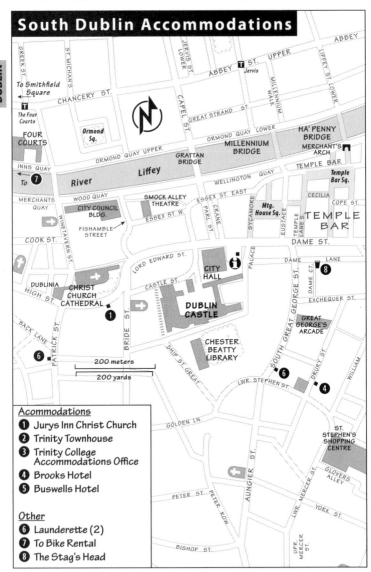

South Dublin Accommodations

Accommodations
1. Jurys Inn Christ Church
2. Trinity Townhouse
3. Trinity College Accommodations Office
4. Brooks Hotel
5. Buswells Hotel

Other
6. Launderette (2)
7. To Bike Rental
8. The Stag's Head

Leeson Close (a lane off Lower Leeson Street). Its understated elegance is top-notch, with seven rooms in a former coach house and 15 rooms in an adjacent Georgian house; the two buildings are connected by a quiet little garden. Guests appreciate the special touches (such as a sunken living room with occasional peat fires) and outstanding breakfasts served in a classy glass atrium (family room, limited parking, 31 Leeson Close, +353 1 676 5011, www. number31.ie, stay@number31.ie).

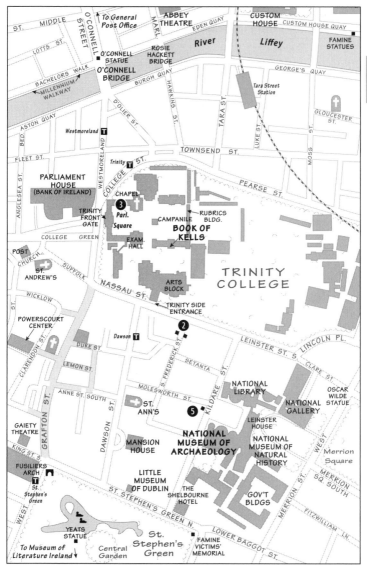

$$$$ The Schoolhouse Hotel taught as many as 300 students in its heyday (1861-1969) and was in the middle of the street fight that was the 1916 Easter Rising. Now it's a serene hideout with 31 pristine rooms and a fine restaurant (breakfast extra, elevator, book early, 2 Northumberland Road, +353 1 667 5014, www. schoolhouse.ie, reservations@schoolhouse.ie).

$$$$ Mespil Hotel is a huge, modern, business-class hotel renting 260 four-star rooms with all the comforts (breakfast extra,

DUBLIN

Southeast Dublin

Accommodations
1. Albany House
2. Fitzwilliam Townhouse
3. Number 31
4. The Schoolhouse Hotel
5. Mespil Hotel
6. Waterloo House
7. Roxford Lodge Hotel

Eateries & Pubs
8. Delahunt
9. Etto
10. Bloom Brasserie & Wine Bar; Zakura Izakaya
11. O'Donoghue's Pub; Doheny & Nesbitt Pub; Toner's Pub
12. Searsons Pub

elevator; small first-come, first-served free parking, 50 Mespil Road, +353 1 488 4600, www.mespilhotel.com, mespil@leehotels. com).

$$$ Waterloo House stands proudly Georgian on a quiet residential street with 19 comfortable rooms on four floors and a pleasant back garden (no breakfast, family rooms, elevator, parking, 8 Waterloo Road, +353 1 660 1888, www.waterloohouse.ie, waterloohouse@eircom.net).

$$$ Roxford Lodge Hotel is in a quiet residential neighborhood a 20-minute walk from Trinity College. This well-managed place has 24 tastefully decorated rooms (a few with hot tubs and saunas—by request). The executive suite is honeymoon-worthy (breakfast extra, family room, elevator, pay parking—limited spots, 46 Northumberland Road, +353 1 668 8572, www.roxfordlodge.ie, reservations@roxfordlodge.ie).

NORTH OF THE RIVER LIFFEY
To locate these hotels, see the "North Dublin" map on page 62.

Near Parnell Square

A swanky neighborhood 250 years ago, this is now workaday Dublin with a steady urban hum, made accessible by LUAS trams.

$$$$ Hotel 7 spruces up an old Georgian property with 51 dark, modern rooms that are refined and stylish. It's worth the comparatively high price for this side of town (breakfast extra, restaurant, 7 Gardiner Row, +353 1 873 7777, www.hotel7dublin.com, info@hotel7dublin.com).

$$$$ Belvedere Hotel, run by the same group as Hotel 7 (described above), has 108 classy, dimly lit, business-comfort rooms (breakfast extra, restaurant, Great Denmark Street, +353 1 873 7700, www.belvederehotel.ie, reservations@belvederehotel.ie).

$$$$ The Castle Hotel is a formerly grand but still-comfortable Georgian establishment embedded in the urban canyons of North Dublin. A half-block east of the Garden of Remembrance, it has aging but pleasant rooms, two restaurants, and the friendly Castle Vaults pub with live music in its basement (breakfast extra, Great Denmark Street, +353 1 874 6949, www.castle-hotel.ie, info@castle-hotel.ie).

$$$$ Jurys Inn Parnell Street has 253 predictably soulless but modern rooms. Its convenient location is just a block west from the north end of O'Connell Street (breakfast extra, pay parking nearby, +353 1 878 4900, www.jurysinns.com, jurysinnparnellst@jurysinns.com).

On Smithfield Square

¢ Generator Hostel provides Dublin's best hostel experience in a clean and stylishly renovated building that was once part of the Jameson Distillery property. The huge 570-bed complex leaves most other hostels looking tired and patched together (breakfast extra, private rooms available, at the base of Jameson Distillery chimney observation tower, +353 1 901 0222, www.generatorhostels.com, dublin@staygenerator.com).

Near Connolly Station and the River Liffey

$$$$ The Address Connolly lies conveniently across the street from Connolly Station and is a fine splurge, with 278 lush, modern rooms. Although the rail tracks run directly behind it, the rooms are effectively soundproofed (breakfast extra, Amiens Street, +353 1 836 3136, www.theaddressconnolly.com, connolly@theaddresscollective.com).

$$$$ Hilton Garden Inn Custom House faces the River Liffey at the edge of the rejuvenated Docklands financial district, with large, modern rooms (breakfast extra, near *Jeanie Johnston* tall ship at 1 Custom House Quay, +353 1 854 1543, www.dublincustomhouse.hgi.com).

Eating in Dublin

While you can get decent pub grub on just about any corner, there's just no pressing reason to eat Irish in cosmopolitan Dublin. In fact, going local these days is the same as going international.

I rank restaurants from $ budget to $$$$ splurge. For more advice on eating in Ireland, including ordering, tipping, and Irish cuisine and beverages, see the "Eating" section of the Practicalities chapter.

Dublin also offers a number of dining-plus-entertainment options, including the Celtic Nights dinner show and the storytelling dinner (listed earlier, under "Entertainment in Dublin"), and a dinner-show version of the Traditional Irish Musical Pub Crawl (listed under "Tours in Dublin," near the beginning of this chapter).

SOUTH DUBLIN EATERIES
"Bib Gourmand" Restaurants

If you want to dine well yet reasonably in Dublin without dressing up, these three restaurants are my favorites. Small, fresh, and untouristy, they've each earned the Michelin "Bib Gourmand" rating for their casual gourmet quality. Menus are creative and modern, dishes are beautifully presented, and they are cozy and romantic. Dinner reservations are a must for these places. Delahunt, south of St. Stephen's Green, is my favorite but is a long walk or cab ride from the center. Pig's Ear and Etto are more central, between Trinity College and St. Stephen's Green.

$$$$ Delahunt is a bright star in a newly vibrant neighborhood. In a long and narrow circa-1906 grocery store, it surrounds its diners with original brass and varnished trappings, and elegant privacy partitions. The waitstaff is friendly and the cuisine—Irish with international influences—is a delight. Dinner is a set five-course menu (Tue-Sat 17:00-21:00, may open for lunch—check their website, closed Sun-Mon, 39 Camden Street Lower, +353 1 598 4880, www.delahunt.ie). For location, see the "Southeast Dublin" map on page 86.

$$$$ The Pig's Ear fills a small and simple, dark-wood-and-candles dining hall. A steep stairway climb above Nassau Street, it overlooks the Trinity College green and wows diners with its modern Irish menu. Choose between the two- and three-course menu (Tue-Sat 17:30-21:00, closed Sun-Mon, 4 Nassau Street, +353 1 670 3865, www.thepigsear.ie).

$$$$ Etto is a small restaurant with tight seating, high volume, and a fun energy. The enticing menu is a fusion of Italian and Irish. I enjoy the view from the bar and would consider reserving a spot there (Tue-Sat 17:00-21:30, open for lunch Fri-Sat, closed Sun-Mon, 2 blocks off St. Stephen's Green, 18 Merrion Row—see

"Southeast Dublin" map on page 86, +353 1 678 8872, www.etto. ie).

Other Restaurants in the Center

$$$ Fallon & Byrne Wine Cellar is a fun surprise. From the big, high-end grocery store on the ground floor, you hike down the stairs to a spacious and welcoming wine cellar with a casual mix of regular and bar-top tables. The wine-friendly menu is international and modern, with €15 main dishes, meat-and-cheese boards, and a fine selection of wine. Your server can give you good wine advice (daily 12:00-22:00, +353 1 472 1012). For a more conventional (and pricier) **restaurant** with modern Irish dishes and good pre-theater menus, climb upstairs (daily 12:00-15:00 & 17:30-21:00, +353 1 472 1000, reservations smart for both, 11 Exchequer Street, www. fallonandbyrne.com).

$$$$ Trocadero is an old-school fixture serving beefy European and modern Irish cuisine to Dubliners interested in a slow, romantic meal. The dressy, red-velvet interior is draped with photos of local actors (Tue-Sat 17:00-22:00, Sun 15:00-19:30, closed Mon, 4 St. Andrew Street, +353 1 677 5545, www.trocadero.ie, Robert).

Fast, Easy, and Cheap

For a quick and healthy lunch, you'll find chain eateries featuring nutritious fare (such as **Sprout & Co** and **Chopped**) all over town. Otherwise, try one of the places listed next.

$ Bewley's Oriental Café is a grand, traditional eatery, centrally located on Grafton Street. Good-value brunch items are offered all day in a wonderful human bustle that epitomizes urban Dublin. Check out the fine Harry Clarke stained-glass windows (against the back wall), fun lunch theater (upstairs), and snack-worthy baked treats (at the takeaway counter around  the corner; Mon-Fri 9:00-17:00, Sat-Sun until 18:00, 78 Grafton Street, +353 1 564 0900). To see what's on at the lunch theater, see www.bewleyscafetheatre.com (€10-15, performances Mon-Sat at 13:00, arrive at 12:45 to settle in and order before the performance begins, +353 86 878 4001).

The Avoca department store has several good, casual food options. The **$$ Avoca Café,** on the second floor, is a cheery eatery thriving with smart local shoppers. They serve healthy foodie plates

DUBLIN

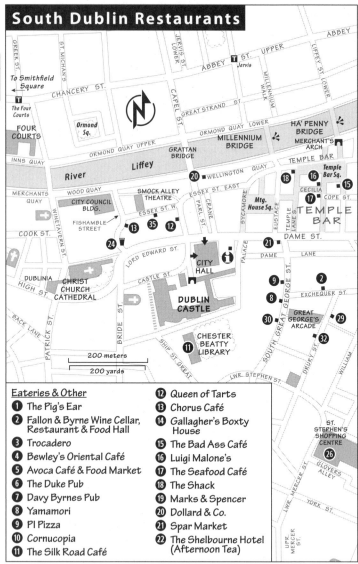

South Dublin Restaurants

Eateries & Other

1. The Pig's Ear
2. Fallon & Byrne Wine Cellar, Restaurant & Food Hall
3. Trocadero
4. Bewley's Oriental Café
5. Avoca Café & Food Market
6. The Duke Pub
7. Davy Byrnes Pub
8. Yamamori
9. PI Pizza
10. Cornucopia
11. The Silk Road Café
12. Queen of Tarts
13. Chorus Café
14. Gallagher's Boxty House
15. The Bad Ass Café
16. Luigi Malone's
17. The Seafood Café
18. The Shack
19. Marks & Spencer
20. Dollard & Co.
21. Spar Market
22. The Shelbourne Hotel (Afternoon Tea)

and great salads (Mon-Sat 9:00-17:00, Sun from 10:00, only tea/coffee and sweets after 16:00). The **$ Avoca Food Market,** in the basement, has a bunch of fresh, ready-made food, including salads, sandwiches, and enticing baked goodies (limited seating—best for takeaway, Mon-Sat 9:00-18:00, Sun from 10:00, 11 Suffolk Street, +353 1 677 4215).

$$ The Duke and **Davy Byrnes,** neighbors on Duke Street, serve reliable pub food. Davy Byrnes feels like a pub-meets-

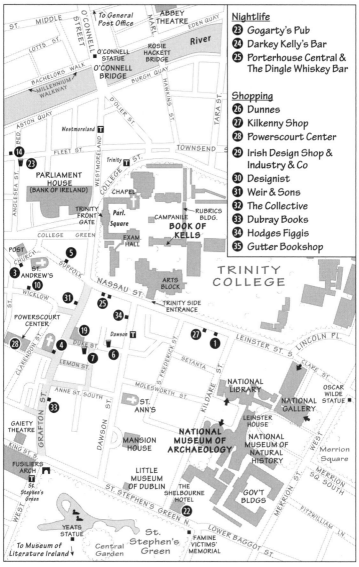

brasserie (at #21, +353 1 677 5217). The Duke has your classic Irish pub ambience (at #8, +353 1 679 9553). Both are favorites for Irish lit fans whose heroes (James Joyce, Brendan Behan, and Patrick Kavanagh) frequented them.

$$$ **Yamamori** is a plain, mellow, and modern Japanese place serving seas of sushi and noodles (daily 12:00-21:00, 73 South Great George's Street, +353 1 475 5001).

$ **PI Pizza** is a hit for its short list of wood-fired, thin-crust

Naples-style pizza. It's mod and fun, and the chef is passionate about quality ingredients (daily 12:00-22:00, 83 South Great George's Street, www.pipizzas.ie).

$ **Cornucopia** is a small, proudly vegetarian ("98% vegan"), counter-service place two blocks off Grafton. It's friendly and youthful, with hearty breakfasts, lunches, and dinner specials, and easy seating (Mon-Sat 9:00-21:00, Sun 10:00-20:30, 19 Wicklow Street, +353 1 677 7583).

Lunch Options near Christ Church Cathedral

$ **The Silk Road Café** at the Chester Beatty Library serves an enticing selection of Middle Eastern and Mediterranean cuisine, including good vegetarian dishes (Thu-Tue until 16:30, Wed until 19:30, on the grounds of Dublin Castle, +353 1 407 0770). While you're there, be sure to pop into the amazing (free) library (see listing earlier, under "Sights in Dublin").

$ **Queen of Tarts,** with nice outdoor seating, does yummy breakfasts, light lunches, sandwiches, and wonderful pastries (Wed-Thu 9:00-17:00, Fri-Sun until 18:00, closed Mon-Tue, just off Dame Street, go 100 yards up from City Hall and left on Cow's Lane, +353 1 633 4681).

$ **Chorus Café** is a friendly and plain little hole-in-the-wall diner serving breakfast, salads, panini, and pastas (daily 8:30-16:00, 7 Fishamble Street, next door to the site of the first performance of Handel's *Messiah*, +353 1 616 7088, Cyrus).

Temple Bar

Temple Bar, while overrun with tourists, has a strange magnetism—you'll likely be drawn here to be part of the scene. It's lined with sloppy eateries charging a premium for their location. These places are open daily for lunch and dinner. If I were to eat in Temple Bar, I'd consider these places:

$$ **Gallagher's Boxty House,** with creaky floorboards and old Dublin ambience, serves stews and corned beef, but the specialty is boxty, the generally bland-tasting Irish potato pancake filled and rolled with various meats, veggies, and sauces (dinner reservations wise, 20 Temple Bar, +353 1 677 2762).

$$ **The Bad Ass Café** serves pizza, burgers, meat and seafood dishes, and salads. There's even a fun kids' menu. Their big patio fronts the Temple Bar action, and there's live music most nights from about 19:00 in the dark, sprawling, pubby interior (9 Crown Alley, +353 1 675 3005).

$$ **Luigi Malone's** has a fun atmosphere and varied menu of pizzas, pastas, burgers, and fajitas (corner of Cecilia and Fownes streets, +353 1 679 2723).

$$$$ **The Seafood Café,** across from Luigi Malone's, is pric-

ey but serves top-quality Irish oysters and fresh seafood dishes (11 Sprangers Yard, +353 1 515 3717).

$$ The Shack, offering traditional Irish, chicken, seafood, and steak dishes, comes with the most sanity of this bunch of Temple Bar eateries (24 East Essex Street, +353 1 679 0043).

Near the Grand Canal

These three places are within a long block of one another in the emerging Grand Canal neighborhood. This area, southeast of St. Stephen's Green (just walk straight out Lower Baggot Street until you cross the canal), feels comfortably workaday with fewer tourists (near the intersection of Baggot Street and Mespil Road). For locations, see the "Southeast Dublin" map on page 86.

$$$ Bloom Brasserie & Wine Bar has a woody, candlelit ambience with beautifully presented dishes based on locally sourced meats and seafood. The menu is modern Irish meets France and changes with the seasons (daily 12:00-14:30 & 17:00-22:30, 11 Upper Baggot Street, +353 1 668 7170).

$$ Searsons Pub, a sprawling neighborhood favorite, is a gastropub known for its lamb, roast meat, and fish specials, with an open kitchen, classy-for-a-sports-bar energy, and friendly service. If there's a horse race or rugby match on, it'll be on the screens here (it's located near the rugby stadium and a betting office). You can escape the clamor out back on the patio (daily 10:00-22:00, 42 Upper Baggot Street, +353 1 660 0330).

$$ Zakura Izakaya is a classy if noisy Japanese place with rice, noodles, and sushi. It's small and tight, like a sushi wine bar (daily 12:00-22:00, 7 Upper Baggot Street, +353 1 563 8000).

HIP AND FUN IN NORTH DUBLIN

For locations, see the "North Dublin" map on page 62.

$$$$ Mr Fox is an elegant and serene little basement operation serving a creative, locally sourced five-course set menu that changes monthly. In summers they open up an outdoor terrace (Tue-Sat 17:00-21:30, also open Sat for lunch 12:00-14:00, closed Sun-Mon, reservations smart especially on weekends, behind the Garden of Remembrance at 38 Parnell Square West, +353 1 874 7778, www.mrfox.ie).

$$$ The Church is a trendy bar/restaurant/beer garden housed in the former St. Mary's Church (which hosted the baptism of Irish rebel Wolfe Tone and the marriage of brewing legend Arthur Guinness). Diners can sit in the choir balcony (with a huge pipe organ) or the ground floor nave, dominated by a long bar. On warm summer nights, the outdoor terrace is packed. Eating here is more about the scene than the cuisine (food served daily 12:00-

21:00, corner of St. Mary's and Jervis Streets, +353 1 828 0102, www.thechurch.ie).

$$ Brannigan's is an inviting family-run traditional pub—it's been a "beer emporium since 1909." Its location, roughly halfway between the Gate and Abbey theaters, makes it convenient for theatergoers and those exploring O'Connell Street (daily 12:00-23:30, 9 Cathedral Street, 50 yards from the Spire, +353 1 874 0137).

$ One Society Café goes for "tasty, healthy, simple" in an unpretentious little space a few blocks east of the Parnell Monument. It's a good, casual place for inventive brunch food and unique specialty pizzas plus occasional pastas (brunch until 15:00, pizza from 16:30; Wed-Sun 10:00-21:00, closed Mon-Tue, 1 Gardiner Street Lower, +353 1 537 5261, www.onesociety.it).

North Quay Docklands Area

This district on the north quay of the River Liffey was a derelict dockland until the late 1980s, when it was transformed into a financial and tech center.

$$$ Harbourmaster Bar and Restaurant occupies the building that once oversaw the ebb and flow of cargo on the surrounding docks. It's a fun place serving good pub grub and higher-end Irish food in a pub on one end and a more peaceful restaurant on the other (Mon-Fri 12:00-23:30, Sat from 13:00, closed Sun, Custom House Dock at George's Dock, look for the little brick building with a clock tower, see map on page 62 for location, +353 1 670 1688, www.harbourmaster.ie).

DELIS, MARKETS, AND FOOD HALLS

If you want to eat fast, cheap, and healthy in the tourist center, several high-end markets offer fresh sandwiches and salad bars. Department stores with fancy grocery sections also generally have what picnickers need: Try **Dunnes** (with several locations) or **Marks & Spencer** (20 Grafton Street). Both of these are open daily until about 20:00 or 21:00.

Unless otherwise noted, the locations of the market halls listed below appear on the map on page 90.

$$ Dollard & Co. is a good market hall with a variety of cuisines, including sushi, Chinese, Thai, pizza, and burgers; there's also a bar. Look over the menus at the central bar, order there, and find a table (your food will be delivered to you). It's popular for breakfast, too. The spacious dining hall has a fun, trendy energy with views of the river (generally daily 8:00-22:00, on the south bank at 2 Wellington Quay, +353 1 616 9606).

$ Fallon & Byrne Food Hall has gourmet grocery items, plus counters with main dishes, desserts, and cheese and charcuterie

(Mon-Sat 8:00-19:00, Sun from 11:00, 11 Exchequer Street, +353 1 472 1010).

$ Spar Market is open 24/7; notice they actually have no front door—it's literally always open, with huge windows overlooking the Dame Street action. Shop for your groceries, then sit down right there and eat them (a block above the Temple Bar commotion at the corner of Dame Street and South Great George's Street, +353 1 633 9070).

$ Baxter & Greene Market Café, north of the river behind the General Post Office, is a handy cafeteria with two locations at the Dunnes in the Ilac Centre (daily 8:30-19:00, Henry Street, one on the ground floor, in Dunnes Food Hall, and the other on the top floor; for location, see map on page 62).

AFTERNOON TEA

$$$$ The Shelbourne Hotel has been a Dublin landmark since 1824, built to attract genteel patrons and Dublin's upper-crust socialites. "Fur coat and no knickers" schlubs can sample the aristocratic good life by enjoying the tradition of afternoon tea in the hotel's Lord Mayor's Lounge (no shorts, tank tops, or T-shirts). The menu is a swirl of finger sandwiches, buttermilk scones, clotted cream, strawberry jam, ginger loaf, and fine coffee...as well as 20-plus varieties of tea (1.75-hour seatings daily at 12:00, 14:30, and 17:00; reservations smart, especially on weekends; 27 St. Stephen's Green, +353 1 663 4500, www.theshelbourne.com).

Dublin Connections

BY PLANE

Dublin Airport has two terminals located an easily walkable 100 yards apart (code: DUB, www.dublinairport.com). Both have ATMs, cafés, Wi-Fi, and luggage storage (www.leftluggage.ie). There is no TI at the airport.

Sleeping at the Airport: A safe bet is the **$$$ Radisson Blu Dublin Airport** (+353 1 844 6000, www.radissonblu.ie).

Linking the Airport and City Center

By Bus: You have two main choices—Dublin Express or Aircoach. Both pick up directly in front of arrivals, at ground level, at both terminals. To check which line works best for your accommodations, check route maps online, or look at the route boards at the stops at the airport (if no one is at the kiosk, ask the driver).

Dublin Express: Bus #782 generally runs along the River Liffey, and includes stops near O'Connell Bridge, Temple Bar, Christ Church, Heuston Station, and Smithfield (runs about 4:00-24:00). Dublin Express bus #784 links the airport to stops near

Merrion Square and Trinity College (runs about 9:00-18:00). Both routes depart about every 30 minutes, and rides take 35-50 minutes (€8 if you pay at kiosk or driver, cheaper if you buy online in advance, +353 1 903 9508, www.dublinexpress.ie).

Aircoach: Bus #700 generally runs a north-south route that follows O'Connell Street down to O'Connell Bridge and St. Stephen's Green (€8 if paying driver, cheaper online, 4/hour, fewer late night, runs about 6:00-1:30 in the morning, +353 1 844 7118, www.aircoach.ie). Aircoach also runs a bus between Dublin Airport and Belfast.

By Taxi: Taxis from the airport into Dublin cost €30-35. Just get in line and tell the dispatcher where you're going. You can also use your Uber app to summon a taxi (because Uber drivers in Ireland must be certified taxi drivers, they will use a meter for your fare).

BY TRAIN OR BUS

The frequencies listed below are for Monday-Saturday (fewer departures on Sunday).

By Train from Dublin's Heuston Station to: Tralee (every two hours, most change in Mallow but one direct evening train, 4 hours), **Ennis** (10/day, 4 hours, change in Limerick, Limerick Junction, or Athenry), **Galway** (8/day, 3 hours), **Westport** (5/day, 3.25 hours). Irish Rail train info: +353 1 836 6222, www.irishrail.ie.

By Train from Dublin's Connolly Station to: Rosslare (3-4/day, 3 hours), Portrush (7/day, 5 hours, transfer in Belfast or Coleraine). The **Dublin-Belfast train** connects the capitals in two hours at 90 mph (8/day). Northern Ireland train info: +44 28 9066 6630, www.translink.co.uk.

By Bus to: Belfast (every 1-2 hours, via Dublin Airport, 2.5 hours), **Trim** (almost hourly, 1 hour), **Ennis** (almost hourly, 5 hours), **Galway** (hourly, 3.5 hours; faster on CityLink—hourly, 2.5 hours, +353 91 564 164, www.citylink.ie), **Westport** (6/day, 6 hours), **Limerick** (7/day, 3.5 hours), **Tralee** (7/day, 6 hours), **Dingle** (4/day, 8.5 hours, transfer at Limerick and Tralee). Bus info: +353 1 836 6111, www.buseireann.ie.

BY CAR

It's best to avoid driving in hectic downtown Dublin. If you plan to drive in Ireland, save your car rental for the countryside. Consider renting a car at the airport, where you'll find all the standard car-rental agencies with longer hours than those in the city and easier access to the M-50.

M-50 Toll Road: Drivers renting a car at Dublin Airport and heading for the countryside can bypass the worst of the big-city traffic by taking the M-50 ring road south or west. The M-50 uses an automatic tolling system called eFlow. Your rental should come with an eFlow tag installed; confirm this when you pick up your car. The €2.10 per-trip toll is automatically charged to the credit card you used to rent the car (www.eflow.ie).

Other Toll Roads: Your rental car's eFlow tag will work only for the M-50 ring road around Dublin. On any other Irish toll roads, you'll need to pay with cash or credit card (about €2/toll). These roads mostly run outward from Dublin toward Waterford, Cork, Limerick, and Galway (roads farther west are free).

CONNECTING IRELAND AND BRITAIN

It's worth spending a few minutes researching your transportation options across the Irish Sea. Most airline and ferry companies routinely offer online discounts. Before sorting out rail/ferry prices with individual companies, try www.tfwrail. wales/ticket-types/sailrail, which deals with several companies and has fares low enough to compete with cheap airlines. Ferries work for rural Wales or Scotland; for everywhere else, fly.

Flights: If you're going directly to London, flying is your best bet. Ryanair and Aer Lingus are the predominant discount carriers, but note that their London-bound flights often land at Luton or Stansted, airports some distance from the city center.

Ferries: Irish Ferries (+353 818 300 400, www.irishferries. com) and Stena Line (+353 1 907 5555, www.stenaline.ie) combine to make eight daily crossings between Dublin Port (two miles east of O'Connell Bridge) and Holyhead, Wales. Most trips take 3.5 hours, but Irish Ferries offers a twice-daily fast boat that makes the trip in 2 hours. Since these boats can fill up on summer weekends, book at least a week ahead during the peak period.

Dublin Bay

Dangling from opposite ends of Dublin Bay's crescent-shaped shoreline, Dun Laoghaire (dun LEERY) and Howth (rhymes with "growth") are two peas in a pod. They offer quiet, cheaper lodging alternatives to Dublin and have easy light-rail access to the city center, just a 25-minute ride away. Dun Laoghaire is bigger and has more going on, while Howth has a sleepier vibe and a fishing fleet.

Dun Laoghaire

Dun Laoghaire is seven miles south of Dublin. This snoozy suburb, with easy connections to downtown Dublin, is a convenient small-town base for exploring the big city.

The Dun Laoghaire harbor was strategic enough to merit a line of martello towers, built in 1804 to defend against an expected Napoleonic invasion (one tower now houses the James Joyce Museum). By the mid-19th century, massive breakwaters were completed to protect the huge harbor. Ferries once sailed regularly from here to Wales (75 miles away), and the first train line in Ireland connected the terminal with Dublin. With those ferries now gone, Dun Laoghaire is much quieter.

GETTING TO DUN LAOGHAIRE

It's easy to get to Dun Laoghaire via DART and Aircoach. But if you really need a taxi, try ABC Taxi service (about €30 to Dublin, €40 to the airport, tel. 01/285-5444).

By DART Commuter Train: The DART commuter train connects to Dublin in 25 minutes (runs about every 10 minutes, daily until about 23:30, €2.65 one-way, €5 round-trip ticket is good same day only, www.irishrail.ie). If you're coming from Dublin, catch a DART train marked *Bray* or *Greystones* and get off at the Sandycove/Glasthule or Dun Laoghaire stop, depending on your B&B's location. Leaving Dun Laoghaire, catch a train marked *Howth* to get to Dublin. Get off at the central Tara Street Station to sightsee in Dublin, or, for train connections north, ride one stop farther to Connolly Station.

By Bus from the Airport: Aircoach bus #703 makes it easy to connect Dun Laoghaire and Dublin Airport (€11 if you buy online, runs every two hours, one-hour ride, see map for stop locations, +353 1 844 7118, www.aircoach.ie).

Parking in Dun Laoghaire: Drivers can leave their cars in Dun Laoghaire and sightsee Dublin by DART. The Pavilion Car Park under the Pavilion Theatre block has a cheap day rate (access facing bay from Queens Road, €6 online advance booking day rate, otherwise €13 for up to 24 hours, +353 1 883 9833, www.parkrite. ie). Note that street parking is limited to three hours (except on Sundays, when it's unlimited and free).

Orientation to Dun Laoghaire

Dun Laoghaire has a coastline defined by its nearly mile-long breakwaters—reaching like two muscular arms into the Irish Sea. The breakwaters are popular for strollers, bikers, birdwatchers, and fishermen.

Helpful Hints: You may find a **seasonal TI** operating from a kiosk near the Dun Laoghaire DART station. For **laundry,** try Park Laundry (full service only, Mon-Fri 8:30-17:30, Sat until 16:30, closed Sun, Upper George's Street, +353 1 551 8977). For the **best views,** hike out to the lighthouse at the end of the East Pier or climb the tight stairs to the top of the stubby martello tower in Sandycove (see next).

Sights in Dun Laoghaire

James Joyce Tower and Museum

This squat martello tower at Sandycove was originally built to repel a possible Napoleonic invasion, but it became famous chiefly because of its association with James Joyce. The great author lived here briefly and made it the setting for the opening of his novel *Ulysses.* The museum's round exhibition space is filled with literary memorabilia, including photographs and rare first editions. For a fine view, climb the claustrophobic, two-story spiral stairwell sealed inside the thick wall to reach the rooftop cannon mount.

Cost and Hours: Free, daily 10:00-18:00, Nov-mid-March until 16:00, the museum is run by volunteers—call ahead to be sure it's open, +353 85 198 2218 or +353 1 280 9265, www.joycetower.ie.

National Maritime Museum of Ireland

Maritime exhibits fill a former church with model steamships, brass fittings, accounts of heroic rescue attempts, and a huge lighthouse optic (lamp lens, installed where the altar once stood). Landlubbers may find it underwhelming.

Cost and Hours: €6, daily 11:00-17:00, Haigh Terrace, +353 1 214 3964, www.mariner.ie.

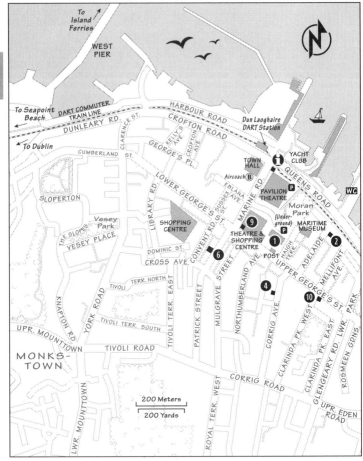

Plays and Concerts

The Pavilion Theatre offers performances in the center of town (box office open Mon-Sat 12:00-17:00, open 2 hours before performances, Marine Road, +353 1 231 2929, www.paviliontheatre.ie).

Swimming

Kids of all ages enjoy swimming at the safe, sandy little cove bordered by rounded rocks beside the martello tower.

Sleeping in Dun Laoghaire

These places lie between the Sandycove/Glasthule and Dun Laoghaire DART stations (check the map to decide which stop to use).

$$$ The **Royal Marine Hotel** is a grand 230-room relic

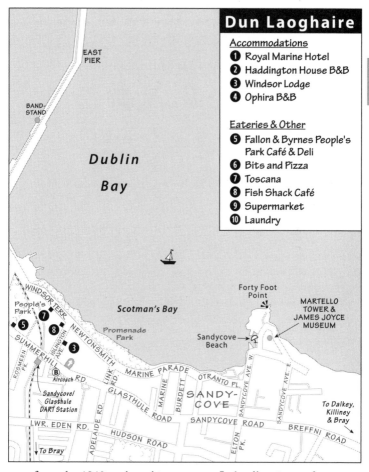

Dun Laoghaire

Accommodations
❶ Royal Marine Hotel
❷ Haddington House B&B
❸ Windsor Lodge
❹ Ophira B&B

Eateries & Other
❺ Fallon & Byrnes People's Park Café & Deli
❻ Bits and Pizza
❼ Toscana
❽ Fish Shack Café
❾ Supermarket
❿ Laundry

from the 1860s, when this town was Ireland's primary ferry port. Its comfortably renovated rooms ooze Old World charm (family rooms, ground-floor pub, on Marine Road, +353 1 230 0030, www.royalmarine.ie, reservations@royalmarine.ie).

$$$ Haddington House rents 40 rooms a block behind the Maritime Museum, with a terrace overlooking the waterfront. They offer afternoon tea in the adjoining parlor, which becomes an elegant cocktail bar in the evening (some rooms with sea views, no kids under 12, bike rental, 9 Haddington Terrace, +353 1 280 1810, http://haddingtonhouse.ie, rooms@haddingtonhouse.ie).

$ Windsor Lodge rents four fresh, inviting rooms on a quiet street a block off the harbor (cash only, 3-night minimum, 3 Islington Avenue, +353 1 284 6952, mobile +353 86 844 6646, www.windsorlodge.ie, windsorlodgedublin@gmail.com, Mary O'Farrell).

$ Ophira B&B is a historic house with four comfortably creaky rooms run by active diver-hiker-biker John O'Connor and his wife, Cathy (family room, parking, 10 Corrig Avenue, +353 1 280 0997, www.ophira.ie, johnandcathy@ophira.ie).

Eating in Dun Laoghaire

George's Street—Dun Laoghaire's main drag, three blocks inland—has plenty of reasonably priced eateries and pubs, many with live music.

$$ Fallon & Byrnes People's Park Café & Deli is your best bet for fine wine and good food in a lovely glassed-in space beside the pleasant People's Park (breakfast from 9:00, lunch from 12:00, Summerhill Road, +353 1 230 3300).

$$ Bits and Pizza is kid-friendly and a good bet for families (daily 12:00-22:00, off George's Street at 15 Patrick Street, +353 1 284 2411).

$$ Toscana, on the seafront, is a popular little cubbyhole, serving hearty Italian dishes and pizza. Its location makes it easy to incorporate into your evening stroll. Reserve for dinner (early-bird specials before 18:30, daily 12:30-22:00, 5 Windsor Terrace, +353 1 230 0890, www.toscana.ie).

$$ Fish Shack Café, on the stroll-worthy waterfront, serves fresh fish dishes to beachcombers (Tue-Sat 12:00-21:00, Sun until 20:00, closed Mon, takeout available, 1 Martello Terrace, +353 1 284 4555).

Groceries: For picnic shopping, try the **Super Valu** under the Dun Laoghaire Shopping Centre, at the corner of Marine Road and Upper George's Street (Mon-Sat 8:00-21:00, Sun 9:00-19:00).

In Glasthule: Called simply "the village" locally, Glasthule is just down the street from the Sandycove/Glasthule DART station and has an array of fun, hardworking little restaurants.

Howth

Eight miles north of Dublin, Howth rests on a teardrop-shaped peninsula that pokes the Irish Sea. Its active harbor chugs with fishing boats earnestly bringing in the daily catch, and seals trolling for scraps. Weary Dubliners come here for refreshing coastal cliff walks. Located at the north terminus of the DART commuter line, Howth makes a good place for travelers to settle in, with easy connec-

tions to Dublin for sightseeing. But there are only a couple centrally located and worthwhile lodging options.

Howth was once an important gateway to Dublin. Near the neck of the peninsula is the suburb of Clontarf, where Irish High King Brian Boru defeated the last concerted Viking attack in 1014. Eight hundred years later, a squat martello tower was built on a bluff above Howth's harbor to defend it from a Napoleonic invasion that never came. The harbor then grew as a port for shipping from Liverpool and Wales. It was eventually eclipsed by Dun Laoghaire, which was first to gain rail access. Irish rebels smuggled German-supplied guns into Ireland via Howth in 1914, making the 1916 Easter Rising possible. Soon after, Howth became a favorite safe-house refuge for rebel mastermind Michael Collins. These days, this is a pleasant coastal hamlet.

DUBLIN

GETTING TO HOWTH

The DART light-rail system zaps travelers between Howth and the city (3/hour, 25 minutes, daily until about 23:30, €2.65 one-way, €5.40 round-trips good same day only, www.irishrail.ie). If you're coming from Dublin, catch a DART train marked *Howth* (not *Howth Junction, Malahide,* or *Drogheda*) and ride it to the end of the line—passing through Howth Junction en route. All trains departing Howth head straight to Dublin's Connolly Station, and then continue on to the Tara and Pearse stations. Get off at Connolly for sightseeing north of the River Liffey or Tara for sightseeing south of the river. Grab a morning train to minimize the jam on sunny summer weekends.

A taxi from the airport takes about 20 minutes and costs about €30.

Orientation to Howth

Howth perches on the north shore of the peninsula and generally divides along the east-west harborfront and the north-south street that winds uphill to the village.

The quarter-mile harborfront promenade stretches from the DART station (in the west) to the martello tower on the bluff (in the east). Dominating the view are two stony piers that clutch like crab claws at the Irish Sea. The West Pier has the fishing action, while the East Pier extends to a stubby 200-year-old lighthouse and views of a rugged nearby island, Ireland's Eye. The village is reached via Abbey Street (becoming Main Street), extending uphill from the harbor near the base of the martello tower bluff. Along the street, you'll find a church, most of the shops and pubs, and a grocery store.

The helpful **TI** is located on the harborfront, in a tiny wooden

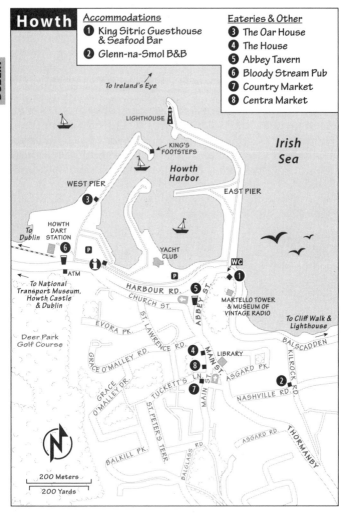

Howth

Accommodations
1 King Sitric Guesthouse & Seafood Bar
2 Glenn-na-Smol B&B

Eateries & Other
3 The Oar House
4 The House
5 Abbey Tavern
6 Bloody Stream Pub
7 Country Market
8 Centra Market

hut on Harbour Road, across from Howth's old courthouse (daily 9:30-17:00, shorter hours off-season, +353 85 858 1695, www. visithowth.ie).

Sights in Howth

Other than coastal walks, sightseeing here pales in comparison to Dublin. Privately owned **Howth Castle** is a big mansion, surrounded by extensive rhododendron gardens. The castle itself can be toured only by appointment (www.howthcastle.ie).

Ye Olde Hurdy Gurdy Museum of Vintage Radio

The three-story martello tower on the bluff overlooking the East Pier is the only sight in Howth worth a glance. Founder Pat Herbert spent decades acquiring this collection of lovingly preserved radios, gramophones, and even a hurdy-gurdy (a crank-action musical oddity)—all of which still work. Check out the radio disguised as a picture frame, which was used by the resistance in occupied France during World War II.

Before leaving the compact bluff, catch the views of the harbor and the nearby island of Ireland's Eye. Spot the distant martello tower on the island's west end and the white guano coating its eastern side, courtesy of a colony of gannets.

Cost and Hours: €5, changeable hours but generally daily 11:00-16:00, Oct-April Sat-Sun only, entry up steep driveway off Abbey Street, +353 86 381 8865.

National Transport Museum of Ireland

Housed in a large warehouse on the castle grounds, this is a dusty waste of time unless you find rapture in old trams and buses (€4, Sat-Sun 14:00-17:00, closed Mon-Fri, +353 85 146 0499, www. nationaltransportmuseum.org).

St. Mary's Abbey

Looming above Abbey Street, the abbey ruins date from the early 1400s. Before that, a church built by Norse King Sitric in 1042 stood at this site. The entrance to the ruins is on Church Street, above the abbey grounds.

East and West Piers

Howth's piers make for mellow strolls after a meal. Poke your head into the various fishmonger shops along the West Pier to see the day's catch. At the end of the pier (on the leeward side), you'll find the footprints of King George IV carved into the stone after his 1821 visit. The East Pier is a quiet jetty barbed with a squat lighthouse and the closest views of the offshore island called Ireland's Eye.

Boat Trips

To get even closer to Ireland's Eye (and its large bird colonies), two excursion operators can either land you on the island or just sail a lap around it. Both operate in summer on demand (daily 10:30-17:00) from the end of the West Pier (€15 to land or €10 to sail around the island; **Island Ferries,** +353 86 845 9154, www. islandferries.net; **Ireland's Eye Ferries,** +353 86 077 3021, www. irelandseyeferries.com).

Dublin Bay Cruises sails the coast between Howth and Dun Laoghaire, stopping in Dublin en route (€25, check website for sailing times and to book, +353 1 901 1757, www.dublinbaycruises. com).

Hiking Trails and Guided Hikes

Trails above the eastern cliffs of the peninsula offer enjoyable, breezy exercise. For a scenic three-hour round-trip, walk past the East Pier and martello tower, following Balscadden Road uphill. You'll soon pass Balscadden House, where writer W. B. Yeats spent part of his youth (watch for plaque on left). A 10-minute stroll beyond that, the road dead-ends, where you'll find the well-marked trailhead and easy-to-follow trail; soon you'll be walking south around the craggy coastline to grand views of the Bailey Lighthouse on the southeast rim of the peninsula. The gate to the lighthouse grounds is always locked, so enjoy the view from afar before retracing your steps back to Howth.

Guided 3.5-hour hiking excursions can be enjoyed with **Hidden Howth Experiences,** whose guides offer insights on the town's Viking history and seafood culture (+353 87 978 1390, www. hiddenhowthexperiences.com). Another option is a four-hour coastal hike with **Howth Adventures** (+353 86 125 0055, www. shaneshowthadventures.com).

Sleeping in Howth

$$$$ King Sitric Guesthouse is Howth's best lodging option and has a fine harborfront seafood bar. It fills the old harbormaster's house with eight well-kept rooms and a friendly staff (East Pier below martello tower, +353 1 832 5235, www.kingsitric.ie, reservations@kingsitric.ie, Aidan and Joan MacManus).

$ Gleann-na-Smol B&B is a homey house with six unpretentious rooms in a quiet setting, a 15-minute walk uphill along the coast behind the martello tower (family room, parking, corner of Nashville and Kilrock Road, +353 1 832 2936, mobile +353 85 758 1083, gleannnasmolbandb@gmail.com, Sean and Margaret Rickard).

Eating in Howth

$$ King Sitric Seafood Bar serves soups, salads, and steak sandwiches—but it's famous for its fish. Sit in the cozy dining room or outside on the covered terrace (Thu-Mon 11:00-23:30, closed Tue-Wed, +353 1 832 5235, www.kingsitric.ie).

$$$ The Oar House sits halfway down the West Pier, serving a variety of fresh fish dishes in a bustling atmosphere (Thu-Sun 12:00-21:00, lunch only Mon-Wed 12:00-16:00, 8 West Pier, +353 1 839 4568).

$$$ The House is the best value up the hill in the village. Here you'll find a comfortable local vibe, a contemporary creative menu, and a rumor that Captain Bligh once lodged here (open daily for breakfast and lunch, 4 Main Street, +353 1 839 6388).

For standard pub grub, try the **$$ Abbey Tavern** up the hill on Abbey Street (occasional trad music and dance, call for schedule, +353 1 839 0307). Another good choice is the **$$ Bloody Stream Pub** in front of the DART station. **The Country Market** sells picnic supplies and has a cheap and friendly tearoom upstairs (daily 7:00-19:00, Thu-Sat until 20:00, Main Street). The **Centra Market** is a block closer to the waterfront (daily until 22:00, Main Street).

DUBLIN

NEAR DUBLIN

Boyne Valley • Trim • Glendalough • Wicklow Mountains • Irish National Stud

Not far from urban Dublin, the stony skeletons of evocative ruins sprout from the lush Irish countryside. The story of Irish history is told by ancient burial mounds, early Christian monastic settlements, huge Norman castles, and pampered estate gardens. In gentler inland terrain, the Irish love of equestrian sport is nurtured in grassy pastures ruled by spirited thoroughbreds. These sights are separated into three regions: north of Dublin (the Boyne Valley, including Brú na Bóinne and the town of Trim), south of Dublin (Powerscourt Estate Gardens, Glendalough, and the Wicklow Mountains), and west of Dublin (the Irish National Stud).

Boyne Valley

The peaceful, green Boyne Valley, just 30 miles north of Dublin, has an impressive concentration of historical and spiritual sights: The enigmatic burial mounds at Brú na Bóinne are older than the Egyptian pyramids. At the Hill of Tara (seat of the high kings of Celtic Ireland), St. Patrick preached his most persuasive sermon. The valley also contains the first monastery in Ireland and several of the country's finest high crosses. You'll see Trim's 13th-century castle—Ireland's biggest—built by Norman invaders, and you can wander the site of the historic Battle of the Boyne (1690), which cemented Protestant British domination over Catholic Ireland until the 20th century.

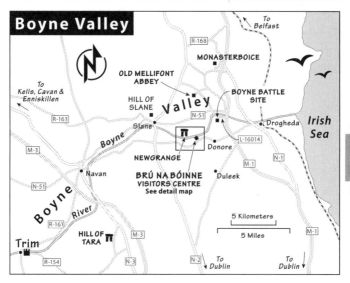

PLANNING YOUR TIME

Of these sights, only Brú na Bóinne is worth ▲▲▲ (and deserves a good three hours). The others, while relatively meager physically, are powerfully evocative to anyone interested in Irish history and culture. If you have a car and get an early start, you could see the entire region in a day.

If you're flying into or out of Dublin but want to avoid the intensity and expense of that big city, consider using Trim as an overnight base (45-minute drive from Dublin's airport) and tour these sights from there.

GETTING AROUND BOYNE VALLEY

The region is a joy by car: All of the described sights are within a 30-minute drive of one another. Though the sights are on tiny roads, they're well marked with brown, tourist-friendly road signs.

It's also possible to get to the Boyne Valley from Dublin with a tour. **Newgrange Tours** visits Brú na Bóinne (including inside the Newgrange tomb), the Hill of Tara, and the Hill of Slane in a seven-hour trip (€55, daily pickup from several Dublin hotels, book direct via website, +353 86 355 1355, www.newgrangetours.com, newgrangetours@gmail.com).

Brú na Bóinne

The famous archaeological site of Brú na Bóinne—"dwelling place of the Boyne"—is also commonly called "Newgrange," after its star attraction. Here you can visit two ▲▲▲ 5,000-year-old passage

NEAR DUBLIN

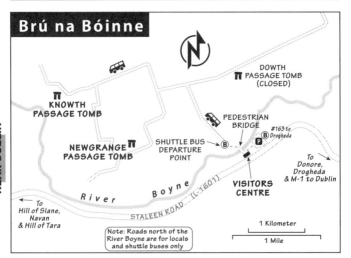

tombs—**Newgrange** and **Knowth** (rhymes with "south"). These are massive grass-covered burial mounds built atop separate hills, with a chamber inside reached by a narrow stone passage. Mysterious, thought-provoking, and mind-bogglingly old, these tombs can give you chills.

Access to Newgrange and Knowth is by guided tour only. Since the Newgrange interior chamber is the most evocative part of the site, I recommend booking the Brú na Bóinne Tour Plus Newgrange Chamber ticket online in advance—the other tours are outside only. Any visit starts with the state-of-the-art visitors center with its excellent exhibit, which provides context to your tomb visits. Then catch your assigned shuttle bus to the tomb sights.

GETTING THERE

By **car,** drive 45 minutes north from Dublin on N-1 toward Drogheda, where signs direct you to the visitors center (watch for *Brú na Bóinne* signs). If you're using GPS, input "Brú na Bóinne visitor center" rather than "Newgrange" to get to your check-in point. Note that you can't drive up to the tombs yourself—you must take a shuttle bus from the visitors center.

Without a car, you can combine **train and taxi** service. First take a train departing Dublin Connolly station around 8:00, then get off in the town of Drogheda an hour later (€20 round-trip; confirm train times at www.irishrail.ie). From Drogheda it's a six-mile taxi ride to the Brú na Bóinne visitors center (approximately €15 one-way).

The **bus** is also an option, either with the Newgrange Tours day trip described earlier in "Getting Around Boyne Valley" or via public transit: Take bus #100x from Dublin to Drogheda, then bus

#163 to the visitors center (allow 2 hours each way, check schedules at www.buseireann.ie).

ORIENTATION TO BRÚ NA BÓINNE

Cost: Brú na Bóinne Tour Plus Newgrange Chamber-€18, Newgrange Tour-€10, Knowth Tour-€10, tours (described below) include visitors center exhibit. For visitors center exhibit only, it's €5.

Hours: Daily 9:00-18:30, slightly shorter hours Sept-April, last bus to the tombs leaves two hours before closing, last entry to visitors center 45 minutes before closing.

Information: +353 46 942 3301, www.heritageireland.ie.

Tours: The main Brú na Bóinne Tour (which visits both Knowth and Newgrange), as well as Newgrange's passage (described below) takes about 2.75 hours including the visitors center exhibit; the other tours take about 2 hours. There is no access to Knowth's interior on any tour.

Advance Tickets Recommended: If you want to take the main tour to see Newgrange's interior, it's essential to reserve timed-entry tickets up to three months in advance online at http://brunaboinne.admit-one.eu. Book other tours at least several days in advance in high season.

VISITING BRÚ NA BÓINNE

At the visitors center, check in and spend your waiting time in the excellent exhibition, grabbing lunch in the cheery downstairs cafeteria, and using the WC (there are none at the tomb sites).

Brú na Bóinne Visitors Centre Exhibition

The exhibition introduces you to the Boyne River Valley and its tombs. No one knows exactly who built the 40 burial mounds found in the surrounding hills. Exhibits explore what the lives of these pre-Celtic people might have been like. Tied to the seasons and eking out a livelihood with crude tools of stone, bone, or wood, they still created some intricate art.

Then around 3200 BC, someone had a bold idea. They constructed a chamber of large stones, with a long stone-lined passage leading up to it. They covered it with a huge mound of dirt and rocks in successive layers. Sailing down the Boyne to the sea, they beached at Clogherhead (12.5 miles from here), where they found hundreds of five-ton stones, weathered smooth by the tides. Somehow they transported them back up the Boyne, possibly by tying a raft to the top of the stone so it was lifted free by a high tide. They then hauled these stones up the hill by rolling them atop logs and up dirt ramps, and laid them around the perimeter of the burial mound to hold everything in place. It would have taken anywhere from five years to a generation to construct a single large tomb.

Why build these vast structures? Partially, it was to bury VIPs. A dead king might be carried up the hill to be cremated on a pyre. Then they'd bring his ashes into the tomb, parading by torchlight down the passage to the central chamber. The remains were placed in a ceremonial basin, mingling with those of his illustrious ancestors. The tombs also served an astronomical function; they're precisely aligned to the movements of the sun.

Since the tombs are aligned with the heavens, it begs the question: Were these structures sacred places where primal Homo sapiens gathered to ponder the deepest mysteries of existence?

The exhibition includes a re-creation of the main passage and chamber in Newgrange, as well as a contemporary, simulated interpretation of a ceremony that might have been held inside.

▲▲▲Newgrange

This grassy mound atop a hill is 250 feet across and 40 feet high. Dating from 3200 BC, it's 500 years older than the pyramids at Giza. The base of the mound is ringed by dozens of curbstones, each about nine feet long and weighing five tons.

The entrance facade is a mosaic of white quartz and dark granite. This is a reconstruction done in the 1970s, and not every archaeologist agrees it originally looked like this. Above the doorway is a square window called the roofbox, which played a key role (as we'll see). In front of the doorway lies the most famous of the curbstones, the 10- by 4-foot entrance stone. Its left half is carved with three mysterious spirals, which have become a kind of poster child for prehistoric art.

Most of Newgrange's curbstones have designs carved into them. This was done with super-hard flint tools; the Neolithic ("New Stone Age") people had not mastered metal. The stones feature common Neolithic motifs: not people or animals, but geometric shapes—spirals, crosshatches, bull's-eyes, and chevrons.

Entering the tomb, you walk down a narrow 60-foot passage lined with big boulders. The passage opens into a central room— a cross-shaped central chamber with three alcoves, topped by a 20-foot-high igloo-type stone dome. Bones and ashes were placed here in a ceremonial stone basin, under 200,000 tons of stone and dirt.

While we know nothing of Newgrange's builders, it most certainly was a sacred spot—for a cult of the dead, a cult of the sun, or both. The tomb is aligned precisely east-west. As the sun rises around the shortest day of the year (winter solstice—usually on Dec 21—and two days before and after), a ray of light enters through the roofbox and creeps slowly down the passageway. For 17 minutes, it lights the center of the sacred chamber (your guide will demonstrate this). Perhaps this was the moment when the souls of the dead were transported to the afterlife, via that ray of light. Then the light passes on, and, for the next 361 days, the tomb sits again in total darkness.

▲▲▲Knowth

This site is an impressive necropolis, with one grand hill-topping mound surrounded by several smaller satellite tombs. The central mound is 220 feet wide, 40 feet high, and covers 1.5 acres.

You'll see plenty of mysteriously carved curbstones and new-feeling grassy mounds that you can look down on from atop the grand tomb.

Knowth's big tomb has two passages: one entering from the east, and one from the west. Like Newgrange, it's likely aligned so the rising and setting sun shone down the passageways to light the two interior chambers, but these are aligned to the equinox rather than the solstice. Neither passage is open to the public, but you can visit a room carved into the mound by archaeologists, where a cutaway lets you see the layers of dirt and rock used to build the mound. You also get a glimpse down one of the passages.

The Knowth site thrived from 3000 to 2000 BC. The central tomb dates from about 2000 BC. It was likely used for burial rituals and sun-tracking ceremonies to please the gods and ensure the regular progression of seasons for crops. The site then evolved into the domain of fairies and myths for the next 2,000 years and became an Iron Age fortress in the early centuries after Christ. Around AD 1000, it was an all-Ireland political center, and later, a Norman fortress was built atop the mound. Now, 4,000 years after prehistoric people built these strange tombs, you can stand atop the hill at Knowth, look out over the surrounding countryside, and contemplate the passage of time.

NEAR DUBLIN

More Boyne Valley Sights

▲▲Battle of the Boyne Site

One of Europe's lesser-known battlegrounds (but huge in Irish and British history), this is the pastoral riverside site of the pivotal 1690 battle in which the Protestant British decisively broke Catholic resistance, establishing Protestant rule over all of Ireland and Britain.

Cost and Hours: €5, daily 10:00-17:00, Oct-April until 16:00, last entry one hour before closing, tearoom/cafeteria, +353 41 980 9950, www. battleoftheboyne.ie.

Getting There: The visitors center is on the south bank of the Boyne River, about two miles north of the village of Donore. It's well signposted for drivers from M-1, N-51, or N-2. Once you pass through the main gates, you'll find the visitors center in the mansion a quarter-mile up the driveway.

"Living History" Demonstrations: Occasional afternoon "Living History" demonstrations are a treat for history buffs and photographers, with guides clad in 17th-century garb. You'll get a bang out of the musket loading and firing demo. Or catch the cavalry combat in full gallop and learn that to be an Irish watermelon is to fear the sword. Check the event program online for schedules and additional offerings such as battlefield walks.

Background: It was here in 1690 that Protestant King William III, with his English/Irish/Dutch/Danish/French Huguenot army, defeated his father-in-law—who was also his uncle—Catholic King James II and his Irish/French army. At stake was who would sit on the British throne, who would hold religious power in Ireland, and whether or not French dominance of Europe would continue.

King William's forces, on the north side of the Boyne, managed to fight their way across the river, and by the end of the day, King James was fleeing south in full retreat. He soon left Ireland, but his forces fought on until their final defeat a year later. James II (called "James da Turd" by those who scorn his lack of courage and leadership) never returned, and he died a bitter ex-monarch in France. His "Jacobite" claim to the English throne lived on among Catholics for decades, and was finally extinguished in 1745, when his grandson, Bonnie Prince Charlie, was defeated at the Battle of Culloden in Scotland.

King William of Orange's victory, on the other hand, is still celebrated in Northern Ireland every July 12, with controversial marches by Unionist "Orangemen." The battle actually took place on July 1, but was officially shifted 11 days later when the Gregorian calendar was adopted in 1752. (Even the calendar has been affected by religious strife: Protestant nations were reluctant to use a calendar developed by a Catholic—Pope Gregory in 1582. So England delayed adoption of Gregory's calendar for 170 years.)

The 60,000 soldiers who fought here made this one of the largest battles ever to take place in the British Isles. Yet it was only a side skirmish in an even larger continental confrontation pitting France's King Louis XIV against the "Grand Alliance" of nations threatened by France's mighty military and frequent incursions into neighboring lands.

Louis ruled by divine right, answerable only to God—and James modeled himself after Louis. Even the pope (who could control neither Louis nor James and was equally disturbed by Catholic France's aggressions) backed Protestant King William against Catholic King James—just one example of the pretzel logic that was the European mindset at the time.

The site of the Battle of the Boyne was bought in 1997 by the Irish Office of Public Works, part of the Republic's governmental efforts to respect a place sacred to Unionists in Northern Ireland—despite the fact that the battle's outcome ensured Catholic subordination to the Protestant minority for the next 230 years.

Visiting the Site: The **visitors center** is housed in a mansion built on the battlefield 50 years after the conflict. The exhibits do a good job of illustrating the international nature of the battle and its place in the wider context of European political power struggles. The highlight is a huge battleground model with laser lights that move troops around the terrain, showing the battle's ebb and flow on that bloody day. A 15-minute film running continuously in the former stable house further fleshes out the battle.

As you exit the site to the north (on the L-16014 access road that connects to the main N-51 road), you'll cross the River Boyne on a **metal bridge,** locally referred to as "Old Bridge." This spot is where the most frantic action took place on the day of the battle.

Pull over and gaze at the river. Picture crack Dutch troops (from King William's homeland) marching south in formation. They were the first to cross the river here, while their comrades behind on the north bank covered their exposed position with constant protective fire. Low tides (the sea is only 7 miles downstream) allowed these soldiers to cross the river in water up to their waists. With the gun smoke, weapon fire, and shouts in the close, chaotic combat, it was tough to tell friend from foe. Neither force had standard uniforms, so King William's troops wore sprigs of green while the troops of King James pinned white paper to their coats. Both sides bled red.

▲Hill of Tara

This site was the most important center of political and religious power in pre-Christian Ireland. While aerial views show plenty of mystifying circles and lines, wandering with the sheep among the well-worn ditches and hills leaves you with more to feel than to see. Visits are made meaningful by an excellent 20-minute video presentation and the insightful 20-minute guided walk that usually follows (walk times unpredictable due to frequent big bus tours; call ahead to confirm availability). Wear good walking shoes—the ground is uneven and often wet.

Cost and Hours: Free, includes guided walk (when available) and video in old church in the trees above parking lot; daily 10:00-18:00, last tour at 17:00, from mid-Sept-mid-May access is free but visitors center is closed; WCs in café next to parking lot, +353 46 902 5903, www.heritageireland.ie.

Visiting the Site: You'll see the Mound of Hostages (a Bronze Age passage grave, c. 2500 BC), a couple of ancient sacred stones, a war memorial, and vast views over the Emerald Isle. While ancient Ireland was a pig pile of minor chieftain-kings scrambling for power, the High King of Tara was king of the mountain. It was at this ancient stockade that St. Patrick directly challenged the king's authority. When confronted by the high king, Patrick convincingly explained the Holy Trinity using a shamrock: three petals with one stem. He won the right to preach Christianity throughout Ireland, and the country had a new national symbol.

This now-desolate hill was also the scene of great later events. In 1798, passionate young Irish rebels chose Tara for its defensible position, but were routed by better-organized (and more-sober) British troops. (The cunning British commander had sent three cartloads of whiskey along the nearby road earlier in the day, knowing the rebels would intercept it.) In 1843, the great orator and champion of Irish liberty Daniel O'Connell gathered 500,000 Irish peasants on this hill for his greatest "monster meeting"—a peaceful show of force demanding the repeal of the Act of Union with Britain (kind of the Woodstock of its day). In a bizarre final twist, a small group of British Israelites—who believed they were one of the lost tribes of Israel who had ended up in Britain—spent

1899 to 1901 recklessly digging up parts of the hill in a misguided search for the Ark of the Covenant.

Stand on the Hill of Tara. Think of the history it's seen, and survey Ireland. It's understandable why this "meeting place of heroes" continues to hold a powerful place in the Irish psyche.

Old Mellifont Abbey

This Cistercian abbey (the first in Ireland) was established by French monks who came to the country in 1142 to bring the Irish monks more in line with Rome. (Even the abbey's architecture was unusual, marking the first time in Ireland that a formal, European-style monastic layout was used.) Cistercians lived isolated rural lives; lay monks worked the land, allowing the more educated monks to devote all of their energy to prayer. After Henry VIII dissolved the abbey in 1539, centuries of locals used it as a handy quarry. Consequently, little survives beyond the octagonal lavabo, where the monks would ceremonially wash their hands before entering the refectory to eat. The lavabo gives a sense of the abbey's former grandeur.

The excellent 45-minute tours, available upon request and included in your admission (late May-Aug only), give meaning to what you're seeing. To get a better idea of the extent of the site, check out the model of the monastery in its heyday, located at the back of the small museum next to the ticket desk.

Cost and Hours: €5; daily 10:00-18:00, last entry 45 minutes before closing; from Sept-late May site is free but there are no tours; +353 41 988 0300, www.heritageireland.ie.

Monasterboice

This ruined monastery is visit-worthy for its round tower and its ornately carved high crosses—two of the best such crosses in Ireland. In the Middle Ages, these crosses, illustrated from top to bottom with Bible stories, gave monks a teaching tool as they preached to the illiterate masses. Imagine the crosses in their prime, brightly painted, before years of wind and rain weathered the paint away. Today, Monasterboice is basically an old graveyard.

Cost and Hours: Free and always open.

Visiting the Site: The 18-foot-tall **Cross of Murdock** (Muiredach's Cross, c. 923, named after an abbot) is considered the best high cross in Ireland. The circle—which characterizes the Irish high cross—could represent the perfection of God. Or, to help ease pagans into Christianity, it may represent the sun, which was worshipped in pre-Christian Celtic society. Whatever its symbolic purpose, its practical function was to support the weight of the crossbeam.

Face the cross (with the round tower in the background) and study the carved sandstone. The center panel shows the Last Judgment, with Christ under a dove, symbolizing the Holy Spirit. Those going to heaven are on Christ's right, and the damned are being ushered away by a pitchfork-wielding devil on his left. Working down, you'll see the Archangel Michael weighing souls, as the Devil tugs demonically at the scales; the adoration of the three—or four—Magi; Moses striking the rock to bring forth water; scenes from the life of David; and, finally, Adam, Eve, and the apple next to Cain slaying Abel. Imagine these carvings with their original, colorful paint jobs. Check out the plaque at the base of the nearby tree, which further explains the carvings on the cross.

Find the even-taller cross nearest the tower. It seems the top section was broken off and buried for a period, which protected it from weathering. The bottom part remained standing, enduring the erosive effect of Irish weather, which smeared the once-crisp features.

The door to the round tower was originally 15-20 feet above the ground (accessible by ladder). After centuries of burials, the ground level has risen.

Trim

The sleepy, workaday town of Trim, straddling the River Boyne, is marked by the towering ruins of Trim Castle. Trim feels littered with mighty ruins that seem to say, "This little town was big-time...800 years ago." The tall Yellow Steeple (over the river from the castle) is all that remains of the 14th-century Augustinian Abbey of St. Mary. Not far away, the Sheep's Gate is a humble remnant of the once-grand medieval town walls. Near the town center, the modest, 30-foot-tall Wellington Column honors native son Arthur Wellesley, the First Duke of Wellington (1769-1852), who spent his childhood in Trim, defeated Napoleon at Waterloo, and twice became prime minister.

Trim makes a great landing pad into—or launching pad out of—Ireland. If you're flying into or out of Dublin Airport and don't want to deal with big-city Dublin, this is a perfect alternative—an easy 45-minute, 30-mile drive away. You can rent a car at the airport and make Trim your first overnight base (getting used to driving on the other side of the road in easier country traffic). Or spend your last night here before returning your car at the airport. Weather permitting, my evening stroll makes for a fine first or last night on the Emerald Isle.

Orientation to Trim

Trim's main square is a traffic roundabout, and everything's within a block or two. Most of the shops and eateries are on or near Market Street, along with banks and a supermarket.

TOURIST INFORMATION

The TI is right next to the castle entrance and includes a small, free exhibit on Trim's history (Mon-Thu 10:00-17:00, Fri until 16:30, closed Sat-Sun, Castle Street, +353 46 943 7227). Outside, beneath the castle walls and across the street from the Trim Castle Hotel, you'll find a plaque with photos showing the castle dolled up for the filming of *Braveheart*.

HELPFUL HINTS

Laundry: The launderette is located close to Market Street (Mon-Sat 9:00-13:00 & 13:30-17:30, closed Sun, Watergate Street, +353 86 844 4299).

Taxi: For visits to nearby Boyne sites, **Donie Quinn** can give you a lift (+353 46 943 6009).

Parking: To park on the street or in a public lot, use the pay-and-display parking system (2-hour maximum, Mon-Sat 9:00-18:00, free Sun).

Adventure Tours: The menu at **Boyne Valley Activities** includes kayaking, rafting, and archery excursions (€30 for archery, €30 for "float through time river tour," €50 for kayaking; call ahead to reserve, +353 86 734 2585, www.boynevalleyactivities.ie).

Sights in Trim

▲▲Trim Castle

This is the biggest Norman castle in Ireland. Set in a grassy riverside park at the edge of this sleepy town, its mighty keep towers above a ruined outer wall.
It replaced a wooden fortification that was destroyed in 1173 by Irish High King Rory O'Connor, who led a raid against the invading Normans. The current castle was completed in the 1220s and served as a powerful Norman state-

ment to the restless Irish natives. It remained a sharp barb at the fringe of "the Pale" (English-controlled territory), when English

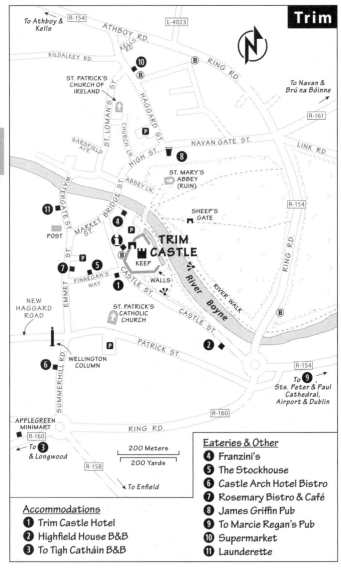

Trim

Accommodations
1 Trim Castle Hotel
2 Highfield House B&B
3 To Tigh Catháin B&B

Eateries & Other
4 Franzini's
5 The Stockhouse
6 Castle Arch Hotel Bistro
7 Rosemary Bistro & Café
8 James Griffin Pub
9 To Marcie Regan's Pub
10 Supermarket
11 Launderette

rule shrank to just the area around Dublin in the 1400s. By that time, any lands farther west were "beyond the Pale."

Cost and Hours: Grounds free, €5 for entrance to keep and required tour; daily 10:00-17:30, Nov-mid-Feb open Sat-Sun only 9:00-17:00, last entry one hour before closing, 45-minute tours run 2/hour but spots are limited and can fill up—so arrive early in peak season, +353 46 943 8619, www.heritageireland.ie.

Visiting the Castle: Today the castle remains an impressive sight—so impressive that it was used in the 1994 filming of *Braveheart* (which was actually about Scotland's—not Ireland's—fight for freedom from the English). The best-preserved walls ring the castle's southern perimeter and sport a barbican gate that contained two drawbridges.

At the base of the castle walls, notice the cleverly angled "batter" wall—used by defenders who hurled down stones that banked off at great velocity into the attacking army. Notice also that the castle is built directly on bedrock, visible along the base of the walls. During sieges, while defenders of other castles feared that attackers would tunnel underground to weaken the defensive walls, that was not an issue here.

The massive 70-foot-high central keep, which is mostly a hollow shell, has 20 sides. This experimental design was not implemented elsewhere because it increased the number of defenders needed to cover all the angles. You can go inside the keep only with the included tour, where you'll start by checking out the cool ground-floor models showing the evolution of the castle. Then you'll climb a series of tightly winding original staircases and modern high catwalks, learn about life in the castle, and end at the top with great views of the walls and the countryside.

Make time to take a 15-minute walk outside, circling the castle walls and stopping at the informative plaques that show the castle from each viewpoint during its gory glory days. Night strollers are treated to views of the castle hauntingly lit in blue-green hues.

Trim Evening Stroll

Given good weather, here's my blueprint for a fine night in Trim. Start the evening by taking the pleasant **River Walk** stroll along the River Boyne from Trim Castle. Cross the wooden footbridge over the river behind the castle and turn right (east). The paved, level trail eventually leads under a modern bridge/overpass and extends a mile along fields that serfs farmed 750 years ago. During the filming of *Braveheart*, Mel Gibson's character met the French princess in her tent in these fields, with the castle looming in the background.

The trail ends in the medieval ruins of **Newtown.** This was indeed once the "new town" (mid-1200s) that sprouted as a religious satellite community to support the political power housed in the castle. Wander the sprawling, ragtag ruins of **Sts. Peter and Paul Cathedral** (1206), once the largest Gothic church in Ireland. Seek out the tomb with a carved lid depicting a medieval lord and lady; this is known locally as the tomb of the "jealous man and woman" (because they do not touch each other). Upon close inspection, you'll notice hundreds of tiny pins in the creases of the carving, left behind by superstitious visitors. Why? If you rub a pin on your stubborn wart and then leave it here...presto: wart-be-gone.

Just beyond the ruins, cross the old Norman bridge to the 13th-century scraps of the **Hospital of St. John the Baptist.** Medieval medicine couldn't have been fun, but this hospital was the best you could hope for back when life was nasty, brutish, and short. Many a knight was spent here.

Cross back over the bridge and stop for a pint at tiny, atmospheric **Marcie Regan's,** one of the oldest pubs in Ireland (an exterior sign calls it "Regan's," but most locals call it "Marcie's"). Explore its dimly lit back rooms. The pub sits beside one of the oldest bridges in Ireland (the one you just crossed).

Then walk back along the river the way you came and have dinner at the recommended **Franzini's** restaurant beside the castle. After dinner, assist your digestion by walking a lap around the castle (beautifully lit at night). End the evening a few blocks away with a pint at the recommended **James Griffin** pub. A fine night 'tis...or 'twas.

Sleeping in Trim

Because Trim is a popular spot for weddings, book as early as possible if you are visiting on a summer weekend.

$$$ Trim Castle Hotel is the town's modern option with 68 immaculate rooms, some with direct views of the castle, and a friendly downstairs pub (family rooms, parking, Castle Street, +353 46 948 3000, www.trimcastlehotel.com, info@trimcastlehotel. com).

$$ Highfield House B&B, across the street from the castle and a five-minute walk from town, is a stately former maternity hospital with hardwood floors and 10 spacious, high-ceilinged rooms (parking, family rooms; above the roundabout where the road from Dublin hits Trim, Castle Street, +353 46 943 6386, mobile +353 86 857 7115, www.highfieldguesthouse.com, info@ highfieldguesthouse.com, Geraldine and Edward Duignan).

$ Tigh Catháin B&B, a countryside B&B a mile southwest of town, has four large, bright, lacy rooms with a comfy, rural feel and organically grown produce at breakfast. Phone ahead for driving directions (cash only, on R-160/Longwood Road, 200 yards past the Applegreen minimart, +353 46 943 1996, mobile +353 86 257 7313, www.tighcathain-bnb.com, tighcathain.bnb@gmail. com, Marie Keane).

Eating in Trim

A country market town, Trim offers basic meat-and-potatoes lunch and dinner options. My first two listings are the only full restaurants in town. Otherwise, the spots along Market Street are friendly, wholesome, and unassuming.

$$$ Franzini's has a fun dinner menu and an excellent location next to the castle. They serve pasta, steak, fish, and great salads in a modern, plush space (Wed-Sat 17:00-21:00, Sun 14:00-20:30, closed Mon-Tue, on French's Lane across from the castle parking lot, +353 46 943 1002).

$$$ The Stockhouse serves hearty steaks and poultry, plus creative desserts. Sit upstairs and take in the history of Trim from the walls while you wait (Wed-Sat 17:00-21:00, Sun from 13:00, closed Mon-Tue, Finnegan's Way, +353 46 943 7388).

$$ The Castle Arch Hotel, popular with locals, serves hearty pub grub at reasonable prices in its bistro on Summerhill Road (daily 12:30-21:00, +353 46 943 1516).

$ Rosemary Bistro & Café is a reliable joint for standard Irish diner food (Mon-Sat 9:30-17:30, closed Sun, 9 Emmet Street, +353 46 948 4814).

Pubs: For a fun pub experience, check out Trim's two best watering holes. The **James Griffin** (on High Street) is full of local characters with traditional Irish music sessions on Monday, Wednesday, and Thursday nights. Locals fill the tiny, low-ceilinged **Marcie Regan's,** a creaky, unpretentious pub at the north end of the old Norman bridge over the River Boyne—it's a half-mile stroll outside town, next to the ruins of Newtown.

Supermarket: The large **SuperValu** is your best bet (long hours daily, on Haggard Street, a short walk from the town center).

Trim Connections

Trim has no train station. Buses from Trim to **Dublin** (almost hourly, 1 hour, www.buseireann.ie) pick you up at the bus shelter next to the TI and castle entrance on Castle Street.

Glendalough and the Wicklow Mountains

The Wicklow Mountains, while only 15 miles south of Dublin, feel remote—enough so to have provided a handy refuge for opponents to English rule. Rebels who took part in the 1798 Irish Rebellion hid out here. The area became more accessible in 1800, when the frustrated British built a military road to help flush out the rebels. Today, this same road—now R-115—takes you through the Wicklow area to Glendalough at its south end. While the valley is the darling of Dublin day-trip tour organizers, for the most part it doesn't live up to the hype. But two blockbuster sights—Glendalough and the Powerscourt Estate Gardens—make a visit worth considering.

GETTING AROUND THE WICKLOW AREA

By car or tour, it's easy. If you lack wheels, take a tour. It's not worth the trouble on public transport.

By Car

It's a delight. Take N-11 south from Dublin toward Bray, then R-117 to Enniskerry, the gateway to the Wicklow Mountains. Signs direct you to the gardens and on to Glendalough. From Glendalough, if you're heading west, you can leave the valley and pick up the highway over the famous but dull mountain pass called the Wicklow Gap.

By Tour from Dublin

Bus Tours: Several companies offer tours around the region. **Wild Wicklow Tours** gives you an entertaining guide who packs every minute of an all-day excursion with information and *craic* (interesting, fun conversation). With a gang of 40 packed into tight but comfortable mountain-gripping buses, the guide kicks into gear from the first pickup in Dublin. Tours cover the windy military road over scenic Sally Gap and the Glendalough monasteries (€33, RS%, runs daily year-round, stop for lunch at a pub—cost not included, several Dublin hotel pickup points, return to Dublin by 18:00, advance booking required, +353 1 280 1899, www.wildwicklow.ie).

Do Dublin Tours offers a trip combining Glendalough, a Wicklow Mountain sheepdog trial, and a visit to Kilkenny aboard a bright green, double-decker bus (€35, daily departure at 8:00, return by 17:00, tours depart from Dublin Bus head office, 59 Upper O'Connell Street, +353 1 844 4265, www.dodublin.ie).

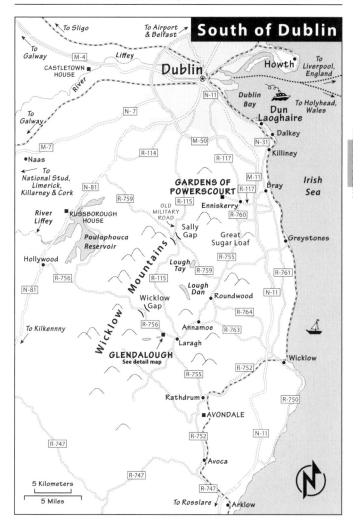

Sights in the Wicklow Area

▲▲Powerscourt Estate Gardens

A mile above the village of Enniskerry, these meticulously kept gardens are Ireland's best, covering 47 acres within a 700-acre estate. The dreamy driveway alone is a mile long. The gardens you see today were created during the Victorian era (1858-1875).

With the impressive summit of the Great Sugar Loaf Mountain as a backdrop, and a fine Japanese garden, Italian garden, and goofy pet cemetery along the way, this attraction provides the scenic greenery I hoped to find in the rest of the Wicklow area. Parts of

The Count of Monte Cristo movie were filmed in this well-watered aristocratic fantasy.

The house was commissioned in the 1730s by Richard Wingfield, first viscount of Powerscourt. The mansion's interior is still only partially restored after a 1974 fire (and available only for special events)—but spend 10 minutes checking out the easy-to-miss film room, which provides a history of the estate and a model of Powerscourt House before the fire.

Cost and Hours: €11.50, daily 9:30-17:30, Nov-Feb until dusk, great cafeteria, +353 1 204 6000, www.powerscourt.com.

Other Sights: Kids may enjoy a peek at the antique dollhouses of the upstairs **Tara's Palace Museum of Childhood** (€5, proceeds go to children's charities, Mon-Sat 10:00-17:00, Sun from 12:00, +353 1 274 8090). Skip the Powerscourt Waterfall (4 miles away).

▲Old Military Road over Sally Gap

This trip is only for those with a car. From the Powerscourt Gardens and Enniskerry, go to Glencree, where you drive the tiny old military road (R-115) over Sally Gap and through the best scenery of the Wicklow Mountains (on Sundays, watch for dozens of bicycle racers). Look for the German military cemetery, built for U-boat sailors who washed ashore in World War II. Near Sally Gap, notice the peat bogs and the freshly cut peat bricks drying in the wind. Many locals are nostalgic for the "good old days," when homes were always peat-fire heated. At the Sally Gap junction, turn left, where a road winds through the vast Guinness estate. Look down on the glacial lake (Lough Tay) nicknamed "Guinness Lake," for its water's resemblance to Ireland's favorite dark-brown stout—the sand of the beach looks like the head of a Guinness beer. From here, the road meanders scenically down into the village of Roundwood and on to Glendalough.

▲▲Glendalough

The steep wooded slopes of Glendalough (GLEN-da-lock, "Valley of the Two Lakes"), at the south end of Wicklow's old military road, hide Ireland's most impressive monastic settlement. Founded by St. Kevin in the sixth century, the monastery flourished (despite repeated Viking raids) throughout the Age of Saints and Scholars until the English destroyed it in 1398. A few hardy holy men continued to live here until it was finally abandoned during the Dissolution of the Monasteries in 1539. But pilgrims kept coming, especially on St. Kevin's Day, June 3. (This might have something to do with the fact that a pope said seven visits to Glendalough had

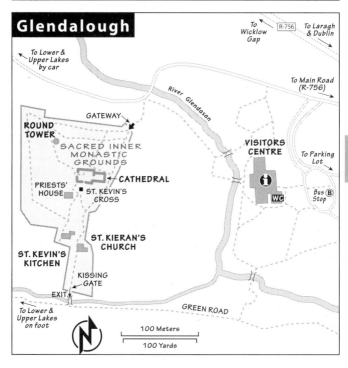

Glendalough

To Wicklow Gap
R-756
To Laragh & Dublin

To Lower & Upper Lakes by car

River Glendasan

To Main Road (R-756)

GATEWAY

ROUND TOWER

SACRED INNER MONASTIC GROUNDS

CATHEDRAL

PRIESTS' HOUSE

ST. KEVIN'S CROSS

VISITORS CENTRE

To Parking Lot

WC

Bus Stop

ST. KIERAN'S CHURCH

ST. KEVIN'S KITCHEN

KISSING GATE

EXIT

To Lower & Upper Lakes on foot

GREEN ROAD

100 Meters

100 Yards

the same indulgence—or forgiveness from sins—value as one visit to Rome.) While much restoration was done in the 1870s, most of the buildings date from the 10th to 12th century.

In an Ireland without cities, these monastic communities were mainstays of civilization. At such remote outposts, ascetics (with a taste for scenic settings, but abstaining from worldly pleasures) gathered to commune with God. In the 12th century, with the arrival of grander monastic orders such as the Cistercians, Benedictines, Augustinians, Franciscans, and Dominicans, and with the growth of cities, these monastic communities were eclipsed. Today, Ireland is dotted with the reminders of this age: illuminated manuscripts, simple churches, carved crosses, and about 100 round towers.

The valley sights are split between the two lakes. The smaller, lower lake is just beyond the visitors center and nearer the best remaining ruins. The upper lake has scant ruins and feels like a state park, with a grassy lakeside picnic area and school groups. Walkers and hikers will enjoy a choice of nine trails of varying lengths through the lush Wicklow countryside (longest loop takes four hours, hiking-trail maps available at visitors center).

Planning Your Time: Summer tour-bus crowds are terrible all day on weekends and 11:00-14:00 on weekdays. If you're there at midday, your best bet is to take the once-daily, 45-minute tour of the site (June-Aug only at 13:30, departs from visitors center). Otherwise, ask if you can tag along with a prebooked tour group's tour. If you're on your own, find the markers that give short descriptions of the ruined buildings.

Here's a good day-plan: Park at the visitors center. Visit the center; take the guided tour if possible; wander the ruins surrounding the round tower on your own (free); or walk the traffic-free Green Road a half-mile to the upper lake, and then walk back to the visitors center along the trail that parallels the public road (an easy, roughly one-mile loop). Or you can drive to the upper lake (skippable, if you're rushed).

Cost and Hours: Free to enter site, €5 for visitors center, pay parking; daily 9:30-18:00, until 17:00 in winter, last entry 45 minutes before closing; +353 404 45352, www.heritageireland.ie.

Visiting Glendalough: Start out at the **Glendalough Visitors Centre,** where a 15-minute video provides a good thumbnail background on monastic society in medieval Ireland. The adjacent museum room features this monastic settlement, with a model that re-creates the fortified village of the year 1050. Interactive exhibits show the contributions these monks made to intellectual life in early medieval Europe (such as illuminated manuscripts and Irish minuscule, a more compact alphabet developed in the seventh century).

When you're ready to visit the site, head out behind the visitors center, cross the bridge over the brook, and follow the lane 100 yards to the original stone **gateway.** From here you enter the sacred inner-monastic grounds that provided sanctuary for anyone under threat. Look for the cross carved into the sanctuary stone in the gateway (at knee level). A refugee had 90 days to live safely within the walls. But on the 91st day, he would be tossed out to the waiting authorities...unless he became a monk (in which case he could live there indefinitely, no matter what his crime).

The graceful **round tower** rises from an evocative tangle of tombstones. Easily the best ruins of Glendalough gather within 100 yards of this famous 110-foot-tall tower. Towers like this (usually 60-110 feet tall with windows facing the four cardinal compass points) were standard features in such monastic settlements. They functioned as bell towers, storage lofts, beacons for pilgrims, and last-resort refuges during Viking raids. (But given enough warning, monks were safer hiding in the surrounding forest.) The towers had a high door with a pull-up lad-

der—both for safety and because a door at ground level would have weakened the tower's foundation. Several ruined churches (10th-12th century) lurk nearby...seek them out.

The **cathedral** is the largest and most central of all the ruins. It evolved over time with various expansions and through the reuse of stones from previous structures. The larger nave came first, and the chancel (up the couple of stairs where the altar later stood) was an addition. The east window faces toward Jerusalem and the rising sun, symbolic of Christ rising from the dead. Under the southern window is a small wall cupboard with a built-in basin. The holy vessels used during Mass were rinsed here so that the holy sacramental water would drain directly into the ground, avoiding any contamination.

Nearby is **St. Kevin's Cross.** At 10 feet tall and carved from a single block of granite, this cross was a statement of utter devotion. (Most other famous Irish high crosses were carved of softer sandstone, allowing their carvers to create more ornate depictions of biblical stories than you'll see here.) According to legend, if you hug this cross and can reach your hands around to touch your fingers on the other side, you'll have your wish granted (and your jealous friends labeling you a knuckle dragger). St. Kevin: the patron saint of dislocated shoulders.

Heading downhill, you'll pass the tiny **priests' house,** which was completely reconstructed (using the original stones) from a 1779 sketch. It might have originally acted as a kind of treasury, housing the relics of St. Kevin.

Farther down, you'll come to perhaps the prettiest structure surviving on the site: **St. Kevin's "kitchen"** (actually a church). Its short round tower appeared to earlier visitors to be a chimney, but its function was always as a belfry. The steeply stacked stone roof conceals a croft (upper story) perhaps used as a scriptorium for copying holy manuscripts. Nearby is the less impressive stone footprint of **St. Kieran's Church,** possibly dedicated to the saint and contemporary of St. Kevin who founded Clonmacnoise Monastery (another scenic sanctuary, on the banks of the River Shannon south of the town of Athlone).

From here, pass through the kissing gate and cross the bridge over the brook. On the other side, if you're short of time, turn left to go back to the visitors center and parking lot. With more time, turn right and explore the lovely tree-shrouded **Green Road,** which leads past the **lower lake** for a half-mile to the **upper lake** as part of a pleasant one-mile loop.

The oldest ruins—scant and hard to find—lie near the upper lake. **St. Kevin's bed** is a cave where the holy hermit-founder of the monastery took shelter. It lies above the left (southern) shore and is visible and reachable only by boat. The story goes that St.

Kevin's devotion was so strong that he would strip off his clothes and jump into thornbushes rather than submit to the pleasures of the flesh. Another tale has him standing in pious stillness with arms outstretched while a bird builds its nest in his hand. If you want a scenic Wicklow walk, begin here.

Irish National Stud

Ireland's famed County Kildare—just west of Dublin—offers the perfect conditions for breeding horses. Its reputation dates all the way back to the 1300s, when Norman war horses were bred here. Kildare's grasslands lie on a bedrock table of limestone, infusing the soil with just the right mix of nutrients for grazing horses. And the nearby River Tully sparkles with high levels of calcium carbonate, essential for building strong bones in the expensive thoroughbreds (some owned by Arab sheikhs) raised and raced here.

In 1900, Colonel William Hall-Walker (Scottish heir to the Johnny Walker distilling fortune) bought a farm on the River Tully and began breeding a line of champion thoroughbreds. His amazing successes and bizarre methods were the talk of the sport. In 1916, the colonel donated his land and horse farm to the British government, which continued breeding horses here. The farm was eventually handed over to the Irish government, which in 1945 created the Irish National Stud Company to promote the thoroughbred industry.

Today, a guided tour of the grounds at the Irish National Stud gives you a fuller appreciation for the amazing horses that call this place home. Animal lovers and horse-racing fans driving between Dublin and Galway can enjoy a couple of hours here, combining the tour with a stroll through the gardens.

GETTING THERE

From M-7, **drivers** take exit #13 and follow the signs five minutes south (don't take exit #12 for the Curragh Racecourse). **Trains** departing Dublin's Heuston station stop at Kildare town (45 minutes). A shuttle bus runs from Kildare's train station to the National Stud (2/hour), or you can take a taxi (about €12-15). One **bus** makes the round-trip from Dublin's Busáras station Mon-Sat (two on Sun). Confirm departure times at the Dublin bus station.

ORIENTATION TO IRISH NATIONAL STUD

Cost: €14, €11 off-season, cheaper online, includes guided tour plus entry to Japanese Gardens, St. Fiachra's Garden, and Horse Museum.

When Irish Horses Are Running

Every Irish town seems to have a betting shop for passionate locals who love to closely follow (and wager on) their favorite horses. A quick glance at the weekend sports sections of any Irish newspaper gives you an idea of this sport's high profile. Towns from Galway to Dingle host annual horse races that draw rabid fans from all over. Interestingly, Irish horse races run the track clockwise (the opposite direction from races in the US).

The five most prestigious Irish races take place at the **Curragh Racecourse,** just south of Kildare town (March-Oct, 1 hour west of Dublin, 10 minutes from the National Stud, www.curragh.ie). Horses have been raced here since 1741. The broad, open fields nearby are where the battle scenes in *Braveheart* were filmed (the neighboring Irish army base provided the blue-face-painted extras).

Hours: Daily 9:00-18:00, off-season from 10:00, closed Nov-Jan, last entry one hour before closing; 45-minute tours depart six times daily in summer, fewer in off-season—check website for current times; +353 45 521 617, www.irishnationalstud.ie.

Eating: There's a decent cafeteria, or bring your own food and eat at a picnic table by the parking lot.

VISITING IRISH NATIONAL STUD

The guided tour begins in the **Sun Chariot Yard** (named for the winner of the 1942 Fillies Triple Crown), surrounded by stables housing pregnant mares. A 15-minute film of a foal's birth runs continuously in a stall in the corner of the yard.

The adjacent **Foaling Unit** is where births take place, usually from February through May. The gestation period for horses is 11 months, with 90 percent of foals born at night. (In the wild, a mare and her foal born during the day would have been vulnerable to predators as the herd moved on. Instead, horses have adapted so that foals are born at night—and are able to keep up with the herd within a few hours.) Eccentric Colonel Hall-Walker noted the position of the moon and stars at the time of each foal's birth, and sold those born under inauspicious astrological signs (regardless of their parents' stellar racing records).

From here, you'll pass a working saddle-making shop and a forge where horseshoes are still hammered out on an anvil.

At the **Stallion Boxes,** you'll learn how stargazing Colonel Hall-Walker installed skylights in the stables—allowing the heavens maximum influence over the destiny of his prized animals. A brass plaque on the door of each stall proudly states the horse's name and its racing credentials. One stall bears the simple word, "Teaser." The unlucky occupant's job is to identify mares in heat... but rarely is the frustrated stallion given the opportunity to breed. Bummer.

After the tour, meander down the pleasant tree-lined **Tully Walk,** with paddocks on each side. You'll see mares and foals running free, with the occasional cow thrown in for good measure (cattle have a calming effect on rowdy horses). To ensure you come home with all your fingers, take full note of the *Horses Bite and Kick* signs. These superstar animals are bred for high spirits—and are far too feisty to pet.

Other Sights: With extra time you can explore three more attractions (all included in entry ticket). The colonel created the tranquil and photogenic **Japanese Gardens** to depict the trials of life (beware the Tunnel of Ignorance). A wander through the more extensive and natural **St. Fiachra's Garden** (the patron saint of gardening) demands more time. Equestrian buffs may want to linger among the memorabilia in the small **Horse Museum,** where you can get a grip on how many hands it takes to measure a horse.

PRACTICALITIES

This section covers just the basics on traveling in the Republic of Ireland (for much more information, see *Rick Steves Ireland*). You'll find free advice on specific topics at RickSteves.com/tips.

MONEY

The Republic of Ireland uses the euro currency: 1 euro (€) = about $1.10. To convert prices in euros to dollars, add about 10 percent: €20 = about $22, €50 = about $55. (Check www.oanda.com for the latest exchange rates.)

You'll use your **credit card** for purchases both big (hotels, advance tickets) and small (little shops, food stands). Visa and Mastercard are universal while American Express and Discover are less common. Some European businesses have gone cashless, making a card your only payment option.

A **"tap-to-pay"** or "contactless" card is the most widely accepted and simplest to use: Before departing, check if you have—or can get—a tap-to-pay credit card (look on the card for the symbol—four curvy lines) and consider setting up your smartphone for contactless payment. Let your bank know that you'll be traveling in Europe, adjust your ATM withdrawal limit if needed, and make sure you know the four-digit PIN for each of your cards, both debit and credit (as you may need to use **chip-and-PIN** for certain purchases). Allow time to receive your PIN by mail.

While most transactions are by card these days, **cash** can help you out of a jam if your card randomly doesn't work, and can be useful to pay for tips and local guides. Wait until you arrive to get euros using your **debit card** (airports have plenty of cash machines). European ATMs accept US debit cards with a Visa or Mastercard logo and work just like they do at home—except they spit out local currency instead of dollars. When possible, withdraw cash from a bank-run ATM located just outside that bank (they usually charge lower fees and are more secure).

Whether withdrawing cash at an ATM or paying with a credit card, you'll often be asked whether you want the transaction processed in dollars or in the local currency. To avoid a poor exchange rate, always refuse the conversion and *choose the local currency*.

Although rare, some US cards may not work at self-service payment machines (such as transit-ticket kiosks, tollbooths, or fuel pumps). Usually a tap-to-pay card does the trick in these situations. Carry cash as a backup and look for a cashier who can process your payment if your card is rejected.

Before you leave home, let your bank know when and where you'll be using your credit and debit cards. To keep your cash, cards, and valuables safe when traveling, wear a **money belt**.

STAYING CONNECTED

The simplest solution is to bring your own device—mobile phone, tablet, or laptop—and use it just as you would at home (following the money-saving tips below). For more on phoning, see RickSteves.com/phoning. For a one-hour talk covering tech issues for travelers, see RickSteves.com/mobile-travel-skills.

To Call from a US Phone: Phone numbers in this book are presented exactly as you would dial them from a US mobile phone. For international access, press and hold the 0 key until you get a + sign, then dial the country code (353 for Ireland) and phone number (omit the initial zero that's used for domestic calls). To dial from a US landline, replace + with 011 (US/Canada international access code).

From a European Landline: Replace + with 00 (Europe international access code), then dial the country code (353 for Ireland) and phone number (omitting the initial zero).

Within Ireland: To place a domestic call (from an Irish landline or mobile), drop the +353 and dial the phone number (including the initial zero).

Tips: If you bring your mobile phone, consider signing up for an international plan; most providers offer a simple bundle that includes calling, messaging, and data.

Use Wi-Fi whenever possible. Most hotels and many cafés offer free Wi-Fi, and you may also find it at tourist information offices (TIs), major museums, public-transit hubs, and aboard trains and buses. With Wi-Fi you can use your phone or tablet to make free or low-cost calls via a calling app such as Skype, WhatsApp, FaceTime, and Google Meet. When you need to get online but can't find Wi-Fi, turn on your cellular network (or turn off airplane mode) just long enough for the task at hand.

Most **hotels** charge a fee for placing calls—ask for rates before

Sleep Code

Hotels in this book are categorized according to the average price of a standard en suite double room with breakfast in high season.

$$$$	**Splurge:**	Most rooms over €170
$$$	**Pricier:**	€130-170
$$	**Moderate:**	€90-130
$	**Budget:**	€50-90
¢	**Backpacker:**	Under €50
RS%	**Rick Steves discount**	

Unless otherwise noted, credit cards are accepted and free Wi-Fi is available. Comparison-shop by checking prices at several hotels (on each hotel's own website, on a booking site, or by email). For the best deal, *book directly with the hotel.* Ask for a discount if paying in cash; if the listing includes **RS%,** request a Rick Steves discount.

you dial. You can use a prepaid international phone card (usually available at newsstands, tobacco shops, and train stations) to call out from your hotel.

SLEEPING

I've categorized my recommended accommodations based on price, indicated with a dollar-sign rating (see sidebar). Book your accommodations as soon as your itinerary is set, especially if you want to stay at one of my top listings or if you'll be traveling during busy times.

Once your dates are set, compare prices at several hotels. You can do this by checking hotel websites and booking sites such as Hotels.com or Booking.com. After you've zeroed in on your choice, **book directly with the hotel itself.** This increases the chances that the hotelier will be able to accommodate special needs or requests (such as shifting your reservation). And when you book on the hotel's website, by email, or by phone, the owner avoids the commission paid to booking sites, giving them wiggle room to offer you a discount, a nicer room, or a free breakfast.

For family-run hotels, it's generally best to book your room directly via email or phone. Here's what they'll want to know: number and type of rooms; number of nights; arrival date; departure date; any special requests; and applicable discounts (such as a Rick Steves discount, cash discount, or promotional rate). Use the European style for writing dates: day/month/year.

Note that to be called a "hotel" in Ireland, a place must have certain amenities, including a 24-hour reception (though this rule is loosely applied). An "en suite" room has a bathroom (toilet and shower/tub) inside the room; a room with a "private bathroom" can

Restaurant Code

Eateries in this book are categorized according to the average cost of a typical main course. Drinks, desserts, and splurge items can raise the price considerably.

$$$$	**Splurge:** Most main courses over €25
$$$	**Pricier:** €20-25
$$	**Moderate:** €15-20
$	**Budget:** Under €15

In the Republic of Ireland, carryout fish-and-chips and other takeout food is **$**; a basic pub or sit-down eatery is **$$**; a gastropub or casual but more upscale restaurant is **$$$**; and a swanky splurge is **$$$$**.

mean that the bathroom is all yours, but it's across the hall.

Some hotels extend a discount to those who pay cash or stay longer than three nights. And some accommodations offer a special discount for Rick Steves readers, indicated in this guidebook by the abbreviation **"RS%."**

Compared to hotels, bed-and-breakfast places give you double the cultural intimacy for half the price. Personal touches, whether it's joining my hosts for afternoon tea or relaxing by a common fireplace at the end of the day, make staying at a B&B my preferred choice. Many B&Bs take credit cards but may add the card service fee to your bill (about 3 percent). If you'll need to pay cash for your room, plan ahead.

A short-term rental—whether an apartment, house, or room in a private residence—is a popular alternative, especially if you plan to settle in one location for several nights. Websites such as Airbnb, FlipKey, Booking.com, and VRBO let you browse a wide range of properties. Alternatively, rental agencies such as InterhomeUSA.com and RentaVilla.com can provide a more personalized service. Ireland's tourism website (www.discoverireland. ie) is also a reliable source for rentals.

EATING

I've categorized my recommended eateries based on the average price of a typical main course, indicated with a dollar-sign rating (see sidebar). The traditional "Irish Fry" breakfast is a hearty way to start the day—with juice, tea or coffee, cereal, eggs, bacon, sausage, a grilled tomato, sautéed mushrooms, and optional black pudding (made from pigs' blood). Toast is served with butter and marmalade. This meal tides many travelers over until dinner.

To dine affordably at classier restaurants, look for "early-bird specials" (sometimes called "pre-theater menus"), which allow you to eat well but early (around 17:30-19:00).

Smart travelers use pubs (short for "public houses") to eat, drink, get out of the rain, and make new friends. Pub grub is Ireland's best eating value (although not every pub serves food). Pubs that are attached to restaurants are more likely to have fresh, made-to-order food. For about $20, you'll get a basic meal in convivial surroundings. The menu is hearty and traditional: stews, soups, fish-and-chips, meat, cabbage, potatoes, boxty (potato pancake filled with fish, meat, or vegetables), and—in coastal areas—fresh seafood such as mackerel, mussels, and Atlantic salmon. Order drinks and meals at the bar, and pay as you order.

When you say "a beer, please" in an Irish pub, you'll get a pint of Guinness. (If you think you don't like Guinness, try it in Ireland—it tastes better in its homeland.) For a cold, refreshing, basic, American-style beer, ask for a lager, such as Harp, or consider craft microbrews. If you want a small beer, ask for a glass, which is a half-pint.

Craic (pronounced "crack"), Irish for "fun" or "a good laugh," means good conversation for the participants. It's the sport that accompanies drinking in a pub. To encourage conversation, stand or sit at the bar.

It's a tradition to buy your table a round, and then for each person to reciprocate. If an Irish person buys you a drink, thank them by saying, *"Go raibh maith agat"* (guh rov mah UG-ut). Offer them a toast in Irish—*"Slainte"* (SLAWN-chuh, the equivalent of "cheers").

Traditional music is alive and popular in pubs throughout Ireland. "Sessions" (musical evenings) may be planned and advertised or impromptu. There's generally a fiddle, a flute or tin whistle, a guitar, a *bodhrán* (goatskin drum), and maybe an accordion or mandolin. Things usually get going at about 21:30—though Irish punctuality is unpredictable. Last call for drinks is at about 23:30.

Tipping: At a sit-down place with table service, tip about 10-12 percent—unless the service charge is already listed on the bill. If you order at a counter, there's no need to tip.

TRANSPORTATION

By Car: It's cheaper to arrange most car rentals from the US. For tips on your insurance options, see RickSteves.com/cdw (note that many credit-card companies do not offer collision coverage for rentals in Ireland). Bring your driver's license.

A car is an expensive headache in Dublin. But if venturing into the countryside, I enjoy the freedom of a rental car for reaching far-flung rural sights. For navigation, the mapping app on your phone works fine. On an all-Ireland trip, you can drive your rental car from the Republic of Ireland into Northern Ireland, but you will pay a drop-off charge (as much as $200) if you return it across the border from where you rented it.

In the Republic of Ireland, you generally can't rent a car if you're 75 or older, and you'll pay extra if you're 70-74.

Remember that the Irish drive on the left side of the road (and the driver sits on the right side of the car). You'll quickly master Ireland's many roundabouts: Traffic moves clockwise, cars inside the roundabout have the right-of-way, and entering traffic yields (look to your right as you merge). Note that road-surveillance cameras strictly enforce speed limits by automatically snapping photos of speeders' license plates, then mailing them a bill.

Many rental-car companies automatically charge for an eFlow pass that electronically pays the toll for Dublin's M50 motorway—ask (see www.eflow.ie).

Local road etiquette is similar to that in the US. Ask your car-rental company for details, or read the Department for Transport's *Highway Code* (www.gov.uk/highway-code), or check the US State Department website (www.travel.state.gov, search for your country in the "Learn About Your Destination" box, then select "Travel and Transportation").

By Train and Bus: A combination of train and bus works best for many routes. You can check train schedules at IrishRail.ie. In the Republic of Ireland, it really pays to buy your train tickets online ahead of time. To see if a rail pass could save you money, check RickSteves.com/rail.

Long-distance buses (called "coaches") are about a third slower than trains, but they're also much cheaper. Bus stations are normally at or near train stations. **Bus Éireann Expressway** is the main bus company in the Republic (www.buseireann.ie); **Translink** serves Northern Ireland (www.translink.co.uk). **Dublin Coach** covers Dublin, Ennis, Killarney, Tralee, Kildare, Kilkenny, Waterford, and Belfast (www.dublincoach.ie, book online at least three hours ahead or pay with credit card onboard).

HELPFUL HINTS

Travel Advisories: Before traveling, check updated health and safety conditions, including restrictions for your destination, on the travel pages of the US State Department (www.travel.state.gov) and Centers for Disease Control and Prevention (www.cdc.gov/travel). The US embassy website for Ireland is also a good source of information (see below).

Covid Vaccine/Test Requirements: It's possible you'll need to present proof of vaccination against the coronavirus and/or a negative Covid-19 test result to board a plane to Europe or back to the US. Carefully check requirements for each country you'll visit well before you depart, and again a few days before your trip. See the websites listed above for current requirements.

Emergency and Medical Help: For any emergency service—

ambulance, police, or fire—call **112** from a mobile phone or land-line. If you get sick, do as the Irish do and go to a pharmacist for advice. Or ask at your hotel for help—they'll know the nearest medical and emergency services.

For **passport problems,** contact the **US Embassy** (in Dublin—by appointment only, +353 1 668 8777, http://ie.usembassy.gov) or the **Canadian Embassy** (in Dublin—by appointment only, +353 1 234 4000, www.canada.ie).

ETIAS Registration: The European Union may soon require US and Canadian citizens to register online with the European Travel Information and Authorization System (ETIAS) before entering any Schengen Zone countries (quick and easy process). For the latest, check www.etiasvisa.com.

Theft or Loss: To replace a passport, you'll need to go in person to an embassy or consulate (see above). Cancel and replace your credit and debit cards by calling these 24-hour US numbers with a mobile phone: Visa (dial +1 303 967 1096), Mastercard (dial +1 636 722 7111), and American Express (dial +1 336 393 1111). From a landline, you can call these US numbers collect by going through a local operator.

File a police report either on the spot or within a day or two; you'll need it to submit an insurance claim for lost or stolen items, and it can help with replacing your passport or credit and debit cards. For more information, see RickSteves.com/help.

Time: Ireland uses the 24-hour clock. It's the same through 12:00 noon, then keep going: 13:00, 14:00, and so on. Ireland, like Great Britain, is five/eight hours ahead of the East/West Coasts of the US (and one hour earlier than most of continental Europe).

Business Hours: In Ireland, most stores are open Monday through Saturday from roughly 10:00 to 17:30 or 18:00, with a late night on Wednesday or Thursday (until 19:00 or 20:00), depending on the neighborhood. On Sundays, sightseeing attractions are generally open (with limited hours), while banks and many shops are closed.

Sightseeing: Many popular sights come with long lines—not to get in, but to buy a ticket. Visitors who buy tickets online in advance (or who have a museum pass covering these key sights) can skip the line and waltz right in. Advance tickets are generally timed-entry, meaning you're guaranteed admission on a certain date and time.

For some sights, buying ahead is required (tickets aren't sold at the sight and it's the only way to get in). At other sights, buying ahead is recommended to skip the line and save time. And for many sights, advance tickets are available but unnecessary: At these uncrowded sights you can simply arrive, buy a ticket, and go in.

Use my advice in this book as a guide. Note any must-see sights that sell out long in advance and be prepared to buy tickets early. If you do your research, you'll know the smart strategy.

Given how precious your vacation time is, I'd book in advance both where it's required (as soon as your dates are firm) and where it will save time in a long line (in some cases, you can do this even on the day you plan to visit).

Holidays and Festivals: Ireland celebrates many holidays, which can close sights and attract crowds (book hotel rooms ahead). For information on holidays and festivals, check Ireland's tourism website: DiscoverIreland.ie. For a simple list showing major—though not all—events, see RickSteves.com/festivals.

Numbers and Stumblers: What Americans call the second floor of a building is the first floor in Europe. Europeans write dates as day/month/year, so Christmas 2023 is 25/12/23. For most measurements, Ireland uses the metric system: A kilogram is 2.2 pounds, a liter is about a quart, and a kilometer is six-tenths of a mile.

RESOURCES FROM RICK STEVES

This Snapshot guide, excerpted from my latest edition of *Rick Steves Ireland,* is one of many titles in my series of guidebooks on European travel. I also produce a public television series, *Rick Steves' Europe,* and a public radio show, *Travel with Rick Steves.* My free online video library, Rick Steves Classroom Europe, offers a searchable database of short video clips on European history, culture, and geography (Classroom.RickSteves.com). My website, RickSteves.com, offers free travel information, a forum for travelers' comments, guidebook updates, my travel blog, an online travel store, and information on European rail passes and our tours of Europe. If you're bringing a mobile device, you can download my free Rick Steves Audio Europe app, which features my two-part Dublin City Walk audio tour, dozens of other audio tours of the top sights in Europe, and travel interviews about Ireland. For more information, see RickSteves.com/audioeurope. You can also follow me on Facebook, Twitter, and Instagram.

ADDITIONAL RESOURCES

Tourist Information: www.discoverireland.ie
Passports and Red Tape: www.travel.state.gov
Packing List: www.ricksteves.com/packing
Travel Insurance: www.ricksteves.com/insurance
Cheap Flights: www.kayak.com or www.google.com/flights
Airplane Carry-on Restrictions: www.tsa.gov
Updates for This Book: www.ricksteves.com/update

HOW WAS YOUR TRIP?

To share your tips, concerns, and discoveries after using this book, please fill out the survey at RickSteves.com/feedback. Thanks in advance—it helps a lot.

INDEX

INDEX

INDEX

South Dublin, 18–33; Trim,
121–122
West Pier (Howth): 105, 106
Whiskey: Celtic Whiskey Shop,
19; Dingle Whiskey Bar, 24,
81; distilleries in The Liberties,
72–73; Old Jameson Distillery,
68; Pearse Lyons, 72; Roe & Co
Whiskey Distillery, 72; Teeling
Distillery, 73
Wicklow Mountains: 124–130; map,
125; tours, 124; transportation,
124

Wilde, Oscar: 22, 25, 52, 53
Wild Wicklow Tours: 124

Y
Yeats, Jack B.: 50
Yeats, William B.: 19, 39, 51, 52, 53,
78, 106
Yellow Steeple (Trim): 118
Ye Olde Hurdy Gurdy Museum of
Vintage Radio (Howth): 105

INDEX

Explore Europe

At ricksteves.com you can browse through thousands of articles, videos, photos and radio interviews, plus find a wealth of money-saving travel tips for planning your dream trip. And with our mobile-friendly website, you can easily access all this great travel information anywhere you go.

TV Shows

Preview the places you'll visit by watching entire half-hour episodes of *Rick Steves' Europe* (choose from all 100 shows) on-demand, for free.

your travel dreams into affordable reality

Radio Interviews

Enjoy ready access to Rick's vast library of radio interviews covering travel tips and cultural insights that relate specifically to your Europe travel plans.

Travel Forums

Learn, ask, share! Our online community of savvy travelers is a great resource for first-time travelers to Europe, as well as seasoned pros.

Travel News

Subscribe to our free Travel News e-newsletter, and get monthly updates from Rick on what's happening in Europe.

Classroom Europe®

Check out our free resource for educators with 500 short video clips from the *Rick Steves' Europe* TV show.

Rick's Free Travel App

Get your FREE **Rick Steves Audio Europe**™ app to enjoy…

- Dozens of self-guided tours of Europe's top museums, sights and historic walks
- Hundreds of tracks filled with cultural insights and sightseeing tips from Rick's radio interviews
- All organized into handy geographic playlists
- For Apple and Android

With Rick whispering in your ear, Europe gets even better.

Find out more at ricksteves.com

Gear up for your next adventure at ricksteves.com

Light Luggage

Pack light and right with Rick Steves' affordable, custom-designed rolling carry-on bags, backpacks, day packs and shoulder bags.

Accessories

From packing cubes to moneybelts and beyond, Rick has personally selected the travel goodies that will help your trip go smoother.

Shop at ricksteves.com

Save time and energy

This guidebook is your independent-travel toolkit. But for all it delivers, it's still up to you to devote the time and energy it takes to manage the preparation and logistics that are essential for a happy trip. If that's a hassle, there's a solution.

Rick Steves Tours

A Rick Steves tour takes you to Europe's most interesting places with great

guides and small groups. We follow Rick's favorite itineraries, ride in comfy buses, stay in family-run hotels, and bring you intimately close to the Europe you've traveled so far to see. Most importantly, we take away the logistical headaches so you can focus on the fun.

Join the fun

This year we'll take thousands of free-spirited travelers—nearly half of them repeat customers—along with us on 50 different itineraries, from Athens to Istanbul. Is a Rick Steves tour the right fit for your travel dreams?

Find out at ricksteves.com, where you can also check seat availability and sign up. Europe is best experienced with happy travel partners. We hope you can join us.

See our itineraries at ricksteves.com

BEST OF GUIDES

Full-color guides in an easy-to-scan format. Focused on top sights and experiences in the most popular European destinations

Best of England
Best of Europe
Best of France
Best of Germany
Best of Ireland
Best of Italy
Best of Scotland
Best of Spain

COMPREHENSIVE GUIDES

City, country, and regional guides printed on Bible-thin paper. Packed with detailed coverage for a multi-week trip exploring iconic sights and venturing off the beaten path

Amsterdam & the Netherlands
Barcelona
Belgium: Bruges, Brussels, Antwerp & Ghent
Berlin
Budapest
Croatia & Slovenia
Eastern Europe
England
Florence & Tuscany
France
Germany
Great Britain
Greece: Athens & the Peloponnese
Iceland
Ireland
Istanbul
Italy
London
Paris
Portugal
Prague & the Czech Republic
Provence & the French Riviera
Rome
Scandinavia
Scotland
Sicily
Spain
Switzerland
Venice
Vienna, Salzburg & Tirol

HE BEST OF ROME

ne, Italy's capital, is studded with
an remnants and floodlit-fountain
res. From the Vatican to the Colos-
s, with crazy traffic in between, Rome
nderful, huge, and exhausting. The
s, the heat, and the weighty history

of the Eternal City where Caesars walked
can make tourists wilt. Recharge by taking siestas, gelato breaks, and after-dark
walks, strolling from one atmospheric
square to another in the refreshing evening air.

ed **Pantheon**—which
est dome until the
ly 2,000 years old
sty over 1,500).

of Athens in the **Vat-**
fies the humanistic
ce.

gladiators fought
nother, entertaining

Rome —

POCKET GUIDES
Compact color guides for shorter trips

Amsterdam
Athens
Barcelona
Florence
Italy's Cinque Terre
London
Munich & Salzburg

Paris
Prague
Rome
Venice
Vienna

SNAPSHOT GUIDES
Focused single-destination coverage

Basque Country: Spain & France
Copenhagen & the Best of Denmark
Dublin
Dubrovnik
Edinburgh
Hill Towns of Central Italy
Krakow, Warsaw & Gdansk
Lisbon
Loire Valley
Madrid & Toledo
Milan & the Italian Lakes District
Naples & the Amalfi Coast
Nice & the French Riviera
Normandy
Northern Ireland
Norway
Reykjavik
Rothenburg & the Rhine
Sevilla, Granada & Southern Spain
St. Petersburg, Helsinki & Tallinn
Stockholm

CRUISE PORTS GUIDES
Reference for cruise ports of call

Mediterranean Cruise Ports
Scandinavian & Northern European
  Cruise Ports

Complete your library with...

TRAVEL SKILLS & CULTURE
*Study up on travel skills and gain
insight on history and culture*

Europe 101
Europe Through the Back Door
Europe's Top 100 Masterpieces
European Christmas
European Easter
European Festivals
For the Love of Europe
Italy for Food Lovers
Travel as a Political Act

PHRASE BOOKS & DICTIONARIES
French
French, Italian & German
German
Italian
Portuguese
Spanish

PLANNING MAPS
Britain, Ireland & London
Europe
France & Paris
Germany, Austria & Switzerland
Iceland
Ireland
Italy
Scotland
Spain & Portugal

Photo Credits

Avalon Travel
Hachette Book Group
1700 Fourth Street
Berkeley, CA 94710

Printed in Canada by Friesens.
7th Edition. First printing January 2023.

ISBN 978-1-64171-527-0

For the latest on Rick's talks, guidebooks, tours, public television series, and public radio show, contact Rick Steves' Europe, 130 Fourth Avenue North, Edmonds, WA 98020, +1 425 771 8303, RickSteves.com, rick@ricksteves.com.

Rick Steves' Europe
Managing Editor: Jennifer Madison Davis
Assistant Managing Editor: Cathy Lu
Editors: Glenn Eriksen, Suzanne Kotz, Rosie Leutzinger, Teresa Nemeth, Jessica Shaw, Carrie Shepherd
Editorial & Production Assistant: Megan Simms
Researchers: Ben Curtis, Cathy Lu
Contributor: Gene Openshaw
Graphic Content Director: Sandra Hundacker
Maps & Graphics: Orin Dubrow, David C. Hoerlein, Lauren Mills, Mary Rostad, Laura Terrenzio

Avalon Travel
Senior Editor and Series Manager: Madhu Prasher
Associate Managing Editor: Jamie Andrade
Editor: Rachael Sablik
Proofreader: Patrick Collins
Indexer: Stephen Callahan
Production: Christine DeLorenzo, Lisi Baldwin, Rue Flaherty, Jane Musser, Ravina Schneider
Cover Design: Kimberly Glyder Design
Maps & Graphics: Kat Bennett

Let's Keep on Travelin'

Your trip doesn't need to end.

Follow Rick on social media!